Yesterday's Milwaukee

Seemann's Historic Cities Series

ROBERT W. WELLS

Yesterday's

MILWAUKEE

Seemann's Historic Cities Series No. 23

E. A. Seemann Publishing, Inc.
Miami, Florida

A dozen public institutions and business firms made photographs available for this book. Their contributions are acknowledged at the end of each caption in abbreviated form, as follows:

Co. Hist. Soc.	Milwaukee County Historical Society
1st Wis.	First Wisconsin National Bank
Journal	The *Milwaukee Journal*
Library	Local history collection, Milwaukee Public Library
Marine	Marine National Exchange Bank, Milwaukee
Muni. Rec.	Milwaukee Municipal Recreation & Adult Education Division
Pabst	Pabst Brewing Company, Milwaukee
Schlitz	Jos. Schlitz Brewing Company, Milwaukee
Univ. Foods	Universal Foods Corporation, Milwaukee
Usinger	Fred Usinger, Inc., Milwaukee
Wauk. C. of C.	Waukesha Chamber of Commerce
Zoo	Milwaukee County Zoo

Library of Congress Cataloging in Publication Data

Wells, Robert W
    Yesterday's Milwaukee.

    (Seemann's historic cities series ; no. 23)
    1. Milwaukee--History--Pictorial works. 2. Milwaukee--Description--Views. I. Title.
F589.M6W42   977.5'95'00222   76-10377
ISBN 0-912458-67-4

Manufactured in the United States of America

This book about the good days that are past
is dedicated to my grandchildren,
Amy Wells, Chip Wells, and Christopher H. Byers,
who represent the future.

Contents

MAP OF
MILWAUKEE
SHOWING LOCATION OF ITS PRINCIPAL
BUILDINGS IN THE SPRING OF 1836.
AS RECOLLECTED BY
D.R ENOCH CHASE, U.B.SMITH & OTHERS.

Indicates Low Lands.

WHEN THE FIRST YANKEE SETTLERS arrived in 1833, much of what became Milwaukee's downtown district was a swamp. Gravel hills left behind by the glaciers were nearby, and the pioneers were fast men with a shovel. By 1836, as the map indicates, part of the tamarack bog west of the river had already been filled. South of Michigan Street on the East Side, there was little dry land except a strip one hundred fifty feet wide along the Lake Michigan shore. Walker's Point, which gave its name to the South Side settlement, was a narrow peninsula which thrust out into the swampy lowlands near the confluence of the Milwaukee and Menomonee rivers. (Marine)

[8]

Preface

THERE ARE two ways to recapture the past. One is with words, the method I attempted in *This Is Milwaukee,* published in 1970. The other is with pictures, the principal means employed in the book you hold in your hand.

Some picture books are meant to be skimmed through lightly, pausing only long enough to study a scene that strikes a familiar chord. I hope you will find many such scenes in *Yesterday's Milwaukee,* but it is not meant strictly for skimming.

This is not merely a haphazard collection of drawings and photographs from earlier days. Viewed in sequence, the pictures with their accompanying text are designed to show how Milwaukee grew from its inauspicious start in a tamarack swamp to the modern era.

But history is more than important people and significant events. The book also tries to capture the flavor of the daily lives led by Milwaukeeans from the city's early days onward. Some of the pictures brought back memories for me—wearing knickers, for example, or cranking the 1927 Chevrolet I drove in high school. I hope they bring back recollections of what life used to be like for you, too, along with a reminder of what we have gained and what we have lost as the past faded imperceptibly, day by day, into the present.

In preparing this book, I collected more than twice as many illustrations as I used. The staff of the Local History Department of the Milwaukee Public Library were particularly helpful, along with Robert G. Carroon of the Milwaukee County Historical Society, and George Wilson of the Municipal Recreation Division.

Among others who were especially cooperative in tracking down and making available photographs and drawings were Ruth Goren, Dick Swearingen, Orval Liljequist, and Paul Woehrmann of the Milwaukee Public Library; Mary Lou Roozen of the Marine National Exchange Bank; Robert Hoag of First Wisconsin National Bank; Tom Spidell and Joseph W. Shoquist of the *Milwaukee Journal;* Grace Ellis of Pabst Brewing Co.; Jules Joseph of

Zigman-Joseph; Joseph O'Connell of the Waukesha Chamber of Commerce; Jack Varick of Barkin-Herman-Solochek & Paulsen; Zoo Director George Speidel; and that prince of Milwaukee *wurstmachers,* Frederick Usinger.

Robert W. Wells

February 1976

Yesterday's Milwaukee

THE FIRST SEVEN YANKEE SETTLERS arrived in Milwaukee just in time to shiver through the winter of 1833. Byron Kilbourn was smarter. He waited until the following spring, when the ice had thawed in the tamarack swamp west of the Milwaukee River, before he reined in his horse to study the prospects.

Kilbourn was a Connecticut native whose family had gone from affluence to poverty after moving to Ohio while he was a boy. The change in fortune left Byron with a single-minded ambition. He wanted to get rich. If he had to bend a few rules to recoup the family wealth, so be it.

In Ohio, Kilbourn worked as a surveyor and helped build canals, but other men reaped the profits. Now he intended to cash in on the opportunities which were opening up in the portion of Michigan Territory that was later to become Wisconsin. The Indians, who had hunted and fished there since shortly after the glaciers retreated ten thousand years before, had been persuaded to sign away all but a few upstate remnants of their ancestral claims. The way was open to settlement. Kilbourn intended to make sure that, when settlers started arriving in large numbers, they'd have to buy the most desirable building sites from him.

He rode around the wilderness, looking for a likely place to start his real estate development. The southwest portion of Wisconsin was already beginning to fill up. Most of the future state's 3,245 residents who were recorded in the 1830 census lived in the lead-mining region across the border from the Illinois boom town of Galena. There were settlements at Prairie du Chien and Green Bay, important outposts of the fur trade in the days of French rule. But Kilbourn was interested in future profits, not recent history. By a considerable feat of imagination, he decided that a city could be made to grow in the marshy land just west of the muddy Milwaukee.

The swamp began just south of Chestnut Street (now Juneau Avenue) and included most of what became the downtown area between Sixth Street and the river. There was a quicksand hole near the present site of the Marc Plaza Hotel. A small island with a single tall elm was located near the future intersection of Second and Clybourn. Much of the remainder of Kilbourn's proposed building development was under water, at least in spring.

The prospects were a little more favorable east of the river, although even there it was hard to walk far in any direction without getting wet feet. Except for a narrow band of sandy shore next to Lake Michigan, travel south of what is now East Michigan Street was mostly by canoe.

If Kilbourn had been given a free choice, he might have chosen the East Side for his community. But he had arrived sixteen years too late for that. Solomon Juneau, the last of a succession of French-Canadian traders who swapped whiskey and other items to Milwaukee Indians for beaver pelts, built a cabin on the east bank in 1818. When it became plain that selling real estate rather than buying furs was the way to get ahead, he was flexible enough to change his line of work. In 1831, two years before the first Yankee settlers arrived, he walked one hundred miles through the woods to Green Bay to take out naturalization papers. That same year, he started to learn English on the theory that the language would soon prove useful in his neighborhood. By the time Kilbourn arrived, Juneau had taken charge of the East Side's real estate development, with Morgan L. Martin of Green Bay as his silent partner. Juneau ran the community's only store and was the acknowledged leader of the little band of settlers in what was unofficially called Juneautown.

When the rivalry between Kilbourntown and Juneau's settlement began, most of the Milwaukee residents were Indians. Their ancestors had lived in the neighborhood for generations. The Menominees gave up their claims to the region in 1831 and the Potawatomis in 1833, but many of them were in no hurry to leave. The new settlers found them generally amiable. Andrew J. Lansing, one of the original seven Yankees, did not hesitate to ask for a meal one night when, returning emptyhanded from a hunting trip, he smelled the aroma of boiling meat as he passed a venerable Indian's hut. Neither man spoke the other's language but the host understood his guest was hungry. He stabbed a morsel from the pot with his knife and presented it to Lansing, who wolfed it down and made signs that he'd like a second piece. After the third helping, the Easterner got to wondering what he was eating. He pointed to the pot and inquired:

"Moo, moo?"

The Indian shook his head.

"Oink, oink?"

Another head shake. Lansing imitated a bear. He neighed like a horse. He pretended to be a mule. Each time his host solemnly indicated that he'd guessed wrong. Finally, the visitor remembered the Indians' favorite ceremonial dish. Feeling a mite queasy, he pointed to the pot and asked:

"Bow, wow?"

The host rose. He walked with dignity to the kettle. He pointed.

"Meow, meow," he explained.

SOLOMON JUNEAU usually gets credit for being Milwaukee's first permanent settler, but his father-in-law, Jacques Vieau, deserves the title. He built a cabin and trading post in what is now Mitchell Park in 1795, twenty-three years before Juneau's arrival. Vieau (the name is sometimes spelled Vieaux) fathered six of his thirteen children while the family was living in Milwaukee. He moved back to Green Bay, however, before the first Yankee settlers arrived. Juneau was there to greet them, and so got credit as the city's founder. (Marine)

[13]

ITINERANT TRADERS had visited Milwaukee since the mid-1700s, some of them settling down there for a time. Like Juneau, most were French-Canadians, but an occasional Englishman also showed up, and there was even a fellow from New Jersey, of all places. Juneau built his cabin and a log building to store beaver pelts and trade goods near the east bank of the Milwaukee River, not far from what became the intersection of Water and Michigan streets. (Marine)

Like Kilbourn, Col. George Walker arrived in 1834. He built a cabin on a peninsula jutting into the swamp a little south of where the Menomonee River emptied into the Milwaukee. This qualified the colonel as founder of Walker's Point and the city's South Side. Walker, whose title was honorary, was a hearty Virginian whose hobby was eating and drinking. He pursued these sports so enthusiastically that he grew into a three-hundred-pounder, an ambulatory advertisement for Milwaukee cooking.

Walker had considerable trouble getting unchallenged title to his land. As a result, Walker's Point lagged behind Juneautown and Kilbourntown. Kilbourn had no such difficulty with his claim. When he filed for three hundred acres west of the river he gave a $100 bribe to a federal clerk, and the transaction went smoothly.

Kilbourn built a cabin at Third and Chestnut (Juneau). Soon there was a thriving little settlement near that corner. Across the river in Juneautown, the cabins were mostly on North Water Street between Michigan and Wisconsin, so the rival settlements were divided not only by the stream but by half a dozen blocks of West Side swamp. Except when the Milwaukee was frozen, there was no easy way to get from one town site to the other, which was exactly how Kilbourn wanted it.

Long-distance travel was easiest by water, giving the East Side settlement near Lake Michigan the advantage. The Milwaukee River had not yet been deepened and straightened to the point where it could handle large ships, so Kilbourn built a small steamer which met the vessels anchored off shore. Its paddle wheels churning, his ship carried new arrivals through the wild rice and cattails along the river to the foot of Oneida (West Wells) Street. From there, they walked north on a wooden sidewalk built on pilings along the swampy west bank until they reached dry land in Kilbourntown. Kilbourn's steamer did not land in Juneautown. If a traveler wanted to go there he had to borrow a canoe or use the log raft Juneau kept tied up next to his trading post as a primitive ferry.

To make sure that settlers arriving on foot or horseback from the south would buy lots in Kilbourntown instead of Juneautown, Kilbourn built a rickety bridge over the Menomonee to connect with a trail leading to Chicago, then a four-day journey by wagon. With such allies as Garret Vliet and Increase Lapham, Kilbourn extended the Chicago road from the bridge to his settlement. Meanwhile, the West Siders platted streets that ended at the Milwaukee River. On the opposite bank, so did the East Siders. To make certain no one supposed the two settlements were one, Kilbourn laid out his east-west streets so they did not match the ones in Juneautown. This decision has caused problems for Milwaukee bridge-builders ever since. When a new span across the river was opened in 1975, for example, it had to be built at an angle, matching its slantwise companion bridges in the downtown.

In Kilbourn's defense, it should be pointed out that he saw no reason why the Milwaukee should ever be bridged.

"My settlements's on the mainland," he said. "Let those Juneautown people worry about bridges if they want to go any way but north."

Even after the two communities became a single village called Milwaukee, the prejudice against spending money on bridges continued west of the river. When three were built anyway, two with public funds, there was grumbling in West Side saloons. Then a

schooner owned by an East Sider smashed into the Spring Street (Wisconsin Avenue) Bridge in 1845, partially wrecking it. That was the final straw for the Kilbourn faction, which decided there was a plot afoot to make them pay for a new bridge.

A Kilbourntown merchant, Moses Kneeland, introduced a resolution at a village board meeting. It called the Chestnut Street bridge an "insupportable nuisance" and demanded that the west half of it be torn down—Kneeland was willing to let the East Siders keep their half of the span.

The East Siders voted down this proposition with the help of Colonel Walker's South Side contingent. The West Siders decided that if they couldn't get rid of the bridge by lawful means, they'd try another way. Early the next morning, a posse was formed, drawing heavily from patrons of the Shanty Tavern and other saloons. Before the East Siders had been roused by the clanging of church bells, the Chestnut Street bridge was wrecked and the mob was busily smashing the one at Oneida Street.

"Cannon" Becker, an East Side saloonkeeper, had custody of the only cannon in town, acquired by Democrats to celebrate election victories. The Democrats had neglected to buy any cannon balls, but a patriotic jeweler donated several leaden clock weights that would serve as well. These were stuffed into the cannon, and the weapon was aimed at Kilbourn's house. Becker was about to touch off the gunpowder when a lawyer, Jonathan Arnold, leaped atop the cannon to make a speech. He pointed out that Byron's dead daughter was lying in state in the Kilbourn parlor. Under the circumstances, cannonading the place with clock weights might seem in bad taste.

So bloodshed was narrowly avoided in what came to be known as the Great Milwaukee Bridge War. That afternoon, the village trustees passed an ordinance assessing a $50 fine and five days in jail for anyone caught wrecking a bridge. Having no further wrecking in mind, the West Siders voted for the measure. A few days later, the trustees voted to rebuild the Chestnut Street bridge. Nothing was said about the one at Oneida.

Meanwhile, however, the East Side was plotting revenge. Kilbourn's faction must be punished. What better way than to cut them off from the advantages of Juneautown, where the jail, post office and several of the leading saloons were located? So a mob gathered at Water and Wisconsin, led by a blacksmith carrying a sledgehammer. A few blows and the Spring Street drawbridge was wrecked, finishing the job done by the ship captain. Then the posse roared south on Water Street to smash a flimsy span that connected the East Side with Walker's Point.

[15]

Now there were no bridges left intact. For months, the only way to get across the river was by boat. A compromise was worked out in 1846, ending the bridge war shortly before Milwaukee was chartered.

The East Siders still held a grudge. They voted 324 to 182 against joining the West Side and Walker's Point to form a single city. But the charter was accepted by a large enough majority in the other two sections, and the measure carried.

The new city was mainly occupied by what were called Yankees, which included anyone born east of Chicago. The principal ethnic minority was the Irish, then heading to America in massive numbers to escape famine at home. The population of Ireland had grown rapidly, reaching 8,250,000 in 1845, the year when the principal source of food was struck by the potato blight. Within two years, an estimated 500,000 people had starved to death or died of typhus or cholera. One of history's great migrations got underway, with many of the Irish heading for America. Their best chance of getting a fresh start was on the frontier, which included Wisconsin Territory.

In Milwaukee, most of the Irish settled on recently filled swamp land south of East Michigan Street in what soon was called the Bloody Third Ward. There was considerable prejudice against them among the Yankees, but the immigrants were tolerated for their willingness to work for low pay, strong backs being a useful asset. The Third Ward settlers spoke what passed for English, but the next big wave of settlers could not. They came from the German states after attempts at liberal reform failed there in 1848. Politics, hard times and opposition to compulsory army service all contributed to the decision to migrate. As a rapidly-growing frontier community where opportunities for newcomers were better than in the settled East, Milwaukee got a disproportionate share of the newly arrived Germans.

[16]

THE MILWAUKEE AND ROCK RIVER CANAL, shown near its northern end, was planned by Kilborn to connect with the Mississippi, permitting shipping to go from Milwaukee to the Gulf of Mexico. Congress authorized sale of 166,000 acres of land to pay for the canal, and a mile of it was built along the west side of the Milwaukee River, drawing its water from a dam. But then the territorial legislature decided to use the land sale proceeds to pay obligations so Wisconsin could enter the union in 1848 debt free. The one-mile canal was used by flour mills and other industries before being filled, paved, and renamed Commerce Street. (Co. Hist. Soc.)

Unlike the Irish, a substantial number of these migrants brought money and marketable skills. Some of the "Forty-Eighters," as the early arrivals were called, were Freethinkers with radical ideas left over from their attempts to change the political system in Europe. But most were good Catholics or Lutherans, more interested in getting along in the new country than in changing its ways.

Some of the German settlers quickly established small businesses which gave employment to later arrivals. The West Side and much of the South Side became predominately Germanic, with Yankees still most numerous on the East Side, except for the Irish enclave in the Third Ward.

The middle Europeans brought with them a taste for beer, a beverage which had not been much admired in Milwaukee before their arrival. A combination brewery and distillery had been established by Richard G. Owens and two other Welshmen at the foot of Huron (Clybourn) Street in 1840, and their Lake Brewery stayed in business for another forty years. But beer did not really catch on until the Germans started making it themselves. By 1850, when Milwaukee's population was 20,061—exactly 9,902 fewer than Chicago's that year—the Wisconsin city had a dozen breweries, nearly all of them operated by Germans. Before long, it also had 255 saloons, along with 47 churches and six temperance societies.

The first brewery destined to survive into a period when beer was Milwaukee's best known product was begun by a German family named Best. Jacob Best, Jr., and a son, Charles, arrived in Milwaukee in 1842 and opened a vinegar works. Two years later they were joined by two other sons and their grandfather, Jacob, Sr., who had been a brewer in Mettenheim. The family bought a site on the Chestnut Street hill. Phillip Best contracted with an ironmonger, A. J. Langworthy, to build a boiler for the new brewery.

No one had ever built a boiler in Milwaukee before, but Langworthy and a workman hammered one together, sitting on the bank of a canal Kilbourn had started in the vain hope of linking Milwaukee with the Mississippi River. When the boiler was finished, Phillip Best walked down the hill with his entire fortune tied up in a red handkerchief. He gave the money to Langworthy as a down payment, telling the ironmonger he'd be back to pick up the boiler when he'd sold enough vinegar to pay the rest of the bill. But Langworthy wasn't a man to stand in the way of progress.

"Take the boiler," he said. "Get to work. Pay as soon as you can."

Best was astonished. These Americans had an unbusinesslike way of conducting their affairs. But he was grateful. He promised Langworthy that the first keg of beer would go to him, adding: "And you shall have free beer as long as you live."

There is a saying around Milwaukee: "We can make it faster than you can drink it." Langworthy lived until he was past eighty, but he never went thirsty.

The Best family enterprise did not concentrate on lager at first. Whiskey sold in saloons for two cents a shot, so beer was not the first choice of the dedicated drinking man. The Empire Brewery turned out rye, bourbon, porter, and ale as well as beer. But as the West Side began filling up with Germans, the market improved for malt beverages, and the distilling branch of the operation was abandoned.

Charles Best left the family enterprise in 1848 to start a brewery of his own, later

THE ORIGINAL BANK BUILDING 1839.

ALEXANDER MITCHELL, a Scotsman, established Milwaukee's first bank in this building shortly after he arrived in 1838 with a carpetbag holding $50,000 of his backers' money. Because banks were then illegal in Wisconsin, Mitchell called his establishment an insurance company. (Marine)

THE WISCONSIN MARINE & Fire Insurance Company, an ancestor of the Marine National Exchange Bank, printed its own currency, including Milwaukee's first $3 bills. Unlike money issued by wildcat banks which sprung up after banking institutions became legal in 1852, these greenbacks were sound and were accepted at face value. (Marine)

selling it to Frederic Miller, who had brought $10,000 in gold with him from Wurttemberg. As Miller's, the brewery is still going strong. Another immigrant, August Krug, started a brewery in 1849 as an offshoot of the small restaurant he ran near Fifth and Chestnut. When he died, his widow married the bookkeeper, Joseph Schlitz, who renamed the brewery accordingly. Control reverted to Krug's nephews, headed by August Uihlein, after Schlitz perished in a shipwreck. But by terms of the will, the brewery's name could not be changed even though descendants of the Uihlein brothers have run the business ever since.

As for the Empire Brewery, begun by the Best family in 1844, it went through several name changes. It was called Best's after Phillip took control from his father and brothers. When he died, leadership passed to a son-in-law, Fred Pabst, former skipper of a lake boat. The captain built the enterprise into what was claimed to be, for a time, the largest brewer of lager in the world, and it was renamed in his honor.

One of the turning points in Milwaukee brewing came in the fall of 1871 when much of Chicago burned down, including most of that city's breweries. Best, Miller, Schlitz, Blatz, and several smaller rivals made sure that no one in Illinois had to go thirsty. By 1872, half of Milwaukee's beer was sold out of town. The city's population then was only 75,000, but it shipped more beer than New York, Philadelphia, or St. Louis. With the newly opened market 90 miles to the south, production soared. Best's, the leading Milwaukee brewery, had produced less than 24,000 barrels in 1869. Five years later, it was turning out 100,000 barrels—more than any other American brewery. Within twenty years it had reached the million-barrel mark.

Milwaukee still makes more beer and its residents loyally drink more of it per capita than any other Americans, but brewing in Beertown has ranked first among the city's industries only during one year, 1890. Even in the early days, before such products as electrical equipment and heavy machinery became the mainstays of Milwaukee's economy, there were other ways to get ahead besides opening a brewery. Tanning, meat packing, brickmaking, and flour milling were among the early industries. For a time, Milwaukee was a leading steel producer, using ore mainly from Iron Ridge, Wisconsin, a few miles to the northwest.

But the fastest way to make a fortune in the 1870s or 1880s in Milwaukee—or to lose one—was to speculate in wheat. Such commodities gamblers as Daniel Newhall, Angus Smith, and Lewis J. Higby bet millions on wheat speculations. Sometimes they won, sometimes they lost, but for a time the local grain trading center, known as the Pit, was one of the world's principal headquarters for grain speculations.

Until the chinch bug arrived to ruin the Wisconsin crop, persuading farmers that dairy cattle were a better bet, the state was a leader in wheat growing. A more important reason for the city's preeminence was its early decision to inspect, weigh, and grade wheat, giving honest measure and making wheat from Milwaukee world renowned for its dependability.

Before 1870, the traders met in hotel lobbies—generally the Newhall House, owned by Daniel. Then a grain trading pit was built, to be replaced in 1880 by an ornate structure called the Chamber of Commerce Building. As the Mackie Building, it's still standing, although few pedestrians passing on East Michigan Street are aware that it was once a headquarters for high stakes speculators.

Three years after the new grain exchange opened, Newhall's hotel burned down. It had long been considered a firetrap by Milwaukeeans, but such distinguished visitors as Gen. Tom Thumb assumed it was safe to stay there. The 25-inch celebrity, who was playing at a local theater, was among those rescued. Most of the forty maids who lived on the top floor were less fortunate. A fireman saved six of them by dragging them across a ladder to the roof of an adjoining building. Several groped their way through smoke-filled passageways that connected the hotel to what is now the Insurance Exchange Building. The rest were among the seventy-one persons who died in the worst fire in Milwaukee's history. Most were burned to death but some were killed when they leaped from upper story windows ahead of the flames.

At the time of the Newhall House fire, Milwaukee's population had risen to 120,000, but it was unusually compact for a city that size. Particularly in German neighborhoods, it was the custom to build two houses on a single narrow lot. One faced the street, the other faced the alley. The rear house was usually built first. When a family prospered, it put up a better dwelling at the front of the lot, renting out the old one or using it for relatives newly arrived from Europe. Even wealthy families often lived within easy walking distance of the husband's job, avoiding the necessity to commute by trolley cars drawn by horses or mules. The Uihlein brothers, for example, built mansions on Galena Street near the Schlitz brewery, making it easy for them to arrive early to keep an eye on the hired help.

The Germanic immigration which had begun forty years earlier was at its height in the 1880s. By then, more than a fourth of Milwaukee's population were German natives, and many others were only a generation or two away from the Fatherland. German dailies had twice as many readers as the three principal English-language newspapers, the *Sentinel,* the *Evening Wisconsin* and a recently-started rival, the *Daily Journal.* Lucius Nieman, owner and editor of the new paper, changed its name to *Milwaukee Journal* only after a German sheet of that name disappeared after a merger.

[20]

EIGHT PIONEER WISCONSIN SETTLERS, along with Jesse Spalding's young son, posed for this photograph in 1867. From left, they are Master Spalding, E. S. Ingalls, Spalding, Nelson Ludington, Daniel Wells, Jr., Dr. J. C. Hall, Abner Kirby, Isaac Stephenson, and Chauncy Simonds. Wells, a lumber baron and real estate speculator, became Milwaukee's richest man. Ike Stephenson, who also made a fortune in lumbering, became a Milwaukee newspaper owner and U.S. senator. (Library)

HARRISON LUDINGTON (left), shown with another pioneer named Talbert C. Dousman, got rich in lumbering and was elected governor. In 1839, while Ludington was minding Solomon Juneau's store, two army officers fired at a deserter from Fort Winnebago who had taken refuge in the shop. The bullet narrowly missed Ludington's brother, Nelson. Harrison grabbed one officer by the throat, bent him over a counter, hit him a mighty blow, wrested the pistol from him, then led a discussion on whether the army officers should be lynched. The officers leaped on their horses and left without waiting to see how the discussion turned out. (Co. Hist. So.)

There was a philosophical split between the Germans and the descendants of the Yankees, who had become a minority in the city they had settled. The Europeans were generally churchgoers but they had little patience with Sunday blue laws that forbade such relaxations as dancing and drinking. The argument over Sunday dance halls was a major political issue in Milwaukee for several decades, with opponents claiming that sin ran rampant at such establishments and making periodic attempts to pass laws to wipe out this threat to womanly innocence. By the 1880s, the Yankees were no longer numerous enough to do much about the saloons except to complain, but in the early days of the European migration attempts had been made to make not only liquor but beer illegal. At one point, Prohibitionists managed to pass a state law making a saloonkeeper legally responsible for any mischief a customer got into during the twenty-four hours after he'd bought a drink. The rule was difficult to enforce but it caused hard feelings. Milwaukee's Germans and Irish, who generally had little contact with each other except as opponents during saloon brawls, combined forces against this threat to the rights of the drinking man. A mob smashed windows and damaged furniture in the Milwaukee home of a state senator, John B. Smith, a leader of the drys. Smith refused to be intimidated, but a year or two later the controversial law was repealed.

Some of the ill feeling between Yankees and immigrants was along religious lines. One of the more interesting of a number of brawls that kept Milwaukee lively during its early years took place in a Methodist church, with Catholics and Methodists smiting each other mightily with railings torn from atop the pews. A prominent Methodist finally restored order by waving a pistol which he had brought with him to the service, just in case.

This dispute came about because the Methodists planned to listen to a speech by a former Trappist monk, who was making a lecture tour to describe to Protestants what he considered the shortcomings of the Catholic church. The speech was finally made, but it took a posse of one hundred newly deputized lawmen and the city's entire volunteer fire department to guard the Free Congregational Church to which the meeting was moved after the Methodist meeting hall was wrecked. Four Catholics were charged with rioting. The jury, composed mainly of Irishmen, decided they couldn't possibly be guilty.

[21]

THE FIRST MILWAUKEE COUNTY COURTHOUSE was built in 1836 on what is now Cathedral Square. Additional offices and a jail (right) were added a few months later. Joseph Scott and Cornelius Bennett broke out of this wooden jailhouse while awaiting trial in April 1837 for the murder of Manitou, an Indian who had violated the rules of their tavern by demanding a free drink. Bennett disappeared for good. Scott was hanged in Indiana for killing his uncle. (Co. Hist. So.)

In later years Milwaukee won a reputation as a notably law-abiding place. But for the first several decades of its existence it was a rough-and-ready community. There was a sheriff to enforce the laws and, after 1855, a police chief. But the law frequently found itself outnumbered.

How widely the causes of mob action varied can be illustrated by two riots in the mid-nineteenth century. One freed an escaped slave from jail. The other resulted in the lynching of a black accused of murdering an Irishman.

Joshua Glover was the slave. He made his way from Missouri to Racine, Wisconsin, in 1854 but was recaptured by his owner, who had him thrown into the flimsy Milwaukee jail until he could be taken South. An Abolitionist editor, Sherman N. Booth, aroused the Milwaukeeans who disapproved of the Fugitive Slave Law, considering it not only immoral but a threat to states' rights. Reinforcements arrived from Racine, led by the Racine County sheriff. The vigilantes demanded that Glover be freed. The request was turned down. So they smashed into the wooden jail, escorted the black out of town, and saw that he got safely away to Canada. Booth and a friend were jailed but the Wisconsin Supreme Court turned them loose, declaring that the Fugitive Slave Law was unconstitutional. The United States Supreme Court reversed this ruling. Wisconsin judges refused to accept this decision and were backed up by the Legislature, which contended that Wisconsin law superseded federal law when there was a conflict between the two. Federal marshalls finally locked up Booth again, but Milwaukee vigilantes broke into the customs house and freed him once more. He departed triumphantly on a speaking tour. It took

[22]

THE CHESTNUT STREET BRIDGE was partially wrecked in the opening phase of the Great Milwaukee Bridge War. The bayou shown on the east side of the stream was later filled in and became River Street, heart of the city's red light district in the period when Milwaukee bragged of being a wide-open town. (Co. Hist. So.)

AFTER THE BRIDGE WAR was settled, the Spring Street bridge was replaced at what is now Wisconsin Avenue. To the left, where Gimbels is now located, was a packing house which threw its wastes into the river, making the spot a fine place to catch fish. (Library)

THE ARTIST took some liberties with this view of the Milwaukee River above the North Avenue
dam—the gondola, for example, was not a customary form of transportation there. But the water was

clean enough to make swimming and boating pleasant, and some of the city's well-to-do families built summer homes along the banks. (Library)

Washington another two months to gather enough armed men so he could be recaptured and put behind bars. On the eve of the Civil War, President Buchanan finally ended the Wisconsin rebellion against federal laws by giving Booth a pardon.

Not long after the editor who became a hero by helping free a slave was turned loose, another mob formed to get two black men, James Shelton and Marshal Clark, out of jail. But this time the jail breakers were not feeling friendly. One of the blacks had killed an Irishman, Darbey Carney, during a street brawl, and public opinion was not in their favor, particularly in the Bloody Third Ward.

Milwaukee's twelve-man police force tried to do its duty, but the rioters threw Chief William Beck and a couple of his men into the gutter, threatened the jailer with a revolver, used an eighteen-foot timber as a battering ram, and burst the jailhouse door open. Angry hands grabbed Clark. While the mob was beating him, Shelton sneaked out an open door, clambered over a twelve-foot fence, and left the vicinity. Clark was dragged to a point near the corner of Water and Buffalo streets and hanged to a piledriver being used to sink footings for a building.

Clark's lynching was widely deplored. Majority opinion felt it would have been better to try him first, then hang him. But the incident caused less talk than a bank riot which also took place in 1861.

Before 1852, banks had not been permitted in Wisconsin. Alexander Mitchell, a Scotsman who later became a railroad president, started one anyway in 1839, but he called it an insurance company. Authorities winked at the fact that it was a bank in everything but name, even issuing its own $3 bills and other currency.

In 1861, when the Civil War began, Mitchell was still running what he now called the Wisconsin Marine and Fire Insurance Company Bank, but he had plenty of competition. Some competitors were wildcat banks which existed mostly to print money, hoping no one would show up to complain that it was worthless. Even more legitimate banks were suddenly in trouble when the Southern states seceded. Most of Wisconsin's paper money was backed by bonds issued by states which left the Union, their shaky financial status having forced those states to pay higher interest rates than Northern ones.

Within a short time, forty-one of the state's one hundred eleven banks were out of business. This was a considerable shock to the Wisconsin economy as well as to those who lost their deposits. The Wisconsin Bankers Association announced that it was guaranteeing currency issued by the seventy survivors.

But then ten of the supposedly solvent seventy closed and the association reneged on its pledge. Workmen who had been paid off in currency of these defunct institutions marched downtown from a German neighborhood on the north side, keeping step to the drums of a brass band. They headed straight for Mitchell's bank.

Showing more courage than good sense, Alex stepped outside to explain the intricacies of banking finance to the group. A paving stone was hurled. If the aim had been better, Mitchell's career might have ended right there. He ducked back inside, scooped up the bank's capital, sneaked out the back door while the mob was breaking down the front entrance, got the money aboard a steamer and sent the ship hurrying out into the bay, where it anchored well off shore until the riot was over.

[26]

THE EMPIRE BREWERY was begun by the Best family in 1844 on the Chestnut Street hill over-looking Kilbourn's original West Side settlement. As the Pabst Brewing Company, it is now the oldest of Milwaukee's three surviving breweries. (Pabst)

Meanwhile, the protesters were wrecking not only Mitchell's bank but the nearby State Bank of Wisconsin, the banking house of J. B. Martin, and an office occupied by Edward P. Allis, later to become the chief founder of the Allis-Chalmers Manufacturing Company. Mayor James Brown called out the Montgomery Guards, a volunteer company that was preparing to head south to fight Confederates as part of the Iron Brigade. The mob drew back when the rookie soldiers arrived. But then it was discovered that the dangerous-looking muskets weren't loaded, no ammunition having been issued just yet. The rioters went back to burning bank furniture, papers and other booty, pausing now and then to heave rocks at the men in uniform. Another military company, Hibbard's Zouaves, finally stopped the riot with a bayonet charge. For the next several weeks, soldiers patrolled downtown streets and loaded cannon were mounted at key intersections.

The companies called out for the bank riot were among numerous amateur military groups formed prior to the Civil War that became the nucleus of regiments that Milwaukee sent South to fight. In prewar days, these military units were split along ethnic, religious, and political lines. There were companies formed by the Whigs, led by the local Yankee aristocracy. There were companies affiliated with the Democrats. There were German companies, Irish companies, "American" companies. And there was mutual suspicion among the rival groups. This led to tragedy just prior to the outbreak of the Civil War.

By 1860, the Whigs had become Republicans and had elected a governor. He decided that there were too many armed Democrats marching around Milwaukee and took away the weapons of an Irish military company with Democratic leanings, the Union Guards. The governor ordered the group to disband. Instead, the Irishmen decided to buy their own rifles. They sold tickets to a lake boat excursion to Chicago to raise the money.

About four hundred Milwaukeeans boarded a steamer, the *Lady Elgin,* for the trip. There was music and eating and drinking, with wives and children joining the men for the holiday. On the return trip, the party was still going strong at midnight when, off Waukegan, Illinois, the *Lady Elgin* collided with the schooner *Augusta* and began to sink.

There were not enough lifeboats on the overcrowded ship, and some of them capsized while being lowered. The shore was a considerable distance away. Several passengers reached it on makeshift rafts constructed from the wooden deck. A few swam to safety despite the chilly water. Others were lucky enough to find places in the lifeboats. But two hundred and twenty-five passengers and crewmen drowned.

Hardly a house in the Third Ward was not in mourning. Funerals continued for weeks as additional bodies washed ashore. An estimated one thousand children were orphaned. With the outbreak of America's bloodiest war the following year, casualty lists became daily reading in the papers, and violent death became common enough. But the night the *Lady Elgin* went down was the mark against which other tragedies were measured for a generation, particularly in Irish neighborhoods.

The principal Milwaukee hero to emerge from the war was Arthur McArthur, Jr., the son of a local judge. He was an eighteen-year-old regimental adjutant when the Twenty-Fourth Wisconsin joined other Union forces in an attack against the supposedly impregnable Confederate position on Missionary Ridge near Chattanooga, Tennessee. Grabbing the colors from an exhausted comrade, McArthur led the charge which sent Southern troops flying. He won the Congressional Medal of Honor and a battlefield promotion to major. Later, as a "boy colonel," he distinguished himself in other actions.

[28]

CHARLES BEST, who broke off from the family brewing enterprise in 1848 to start the Plank Road Brewery on the Watertown Plank Road (now State Street), sold it seven years later to Frederic Miller, who had brought $10,000 in gold with him from Germany. The steps at the left led to caves used to store beer. A summer garden was located on the slope. (Library)

After the fighting ended, McArthur did not go into politics like most other Wisconsin war heroes but stayed in the Army. His son, Douglas, who changed the spelling of the family name to MacArthur, became Milwaukee's most famous contribution to World War II, although when the five-star general returned for a triumphal reception in 1951, it was the first time he'd been back to his old hometown in half a century.

THE JOSEPH SCHLITZ BREWING COMPANY was begun on Chestnut Street (Juneau) by August Krug in 1849. His widow married Schlitz, who renamed the brewery and expanded it to the proportions shown in this early sketch. (Schlitz)

THE FIRST PRACTICAL TYPE-
writer, invented by Christopher Latham
Sholes in 1867, was built in Kleinsteuber's machine shop, located on West
State Street across from the present site
of the *Milwaukee Journal.* Mathias
Schwalbach, a Kleinsteuber mechanic,
did the work. Six years later, Sholes
sold the rights to his invention to E.
Remington & Sons for $12,000, thus
avoiding the chance to become a
millionaire. (Library)

BYRON KILBOURN never got as rich as he had hoped he would, but by 1855 he had prospered to the
point where he spent $18,000 to build an impressive home at what is now the corner of Fourth and
Wisconsin. By the time this photo was taken, the dwelling had been converted into shops. The building
was torn down in 1886 to make way for Espenhain's Department Store. After that establishment went
out of business in the early 1930s, A J. C. Penny outlet was built on the site of Kilbourn's home.
(Library)

IN THIS RARE PHOTOGRAPH from 1861, a portion of the Second Wisconsin Infantry is shown before the original Courthouse in what is now Cathedral Square. The regiment was destined to lose a higher percentage of men in battle than any other in the Union army. Note the gray uniforms, the color supplied to Wisconsin troops until the first Battle of Bull Run (Manassas). Other Northern soldiers began firing at the Second Wisconsin, assuming the men in gray were Confederates. The Second and two other Wisconsin regiments later joined an Indiana regiment and one from Michigan to form the Iron Brigade, which saw some of the heaviest fighting of the war. (Co. Hist. So.)

[31]

ALEXANDER MITCHELL, who built this mansion, was not only Milwaukee's first banker but became president of two railroads nad the city's richest man. The gazebo in the foreground is still there. The house forms part of the Wisconsin Club—known as the Deutscher Club until World War I made a name change advisable. The Milwaukee airport is named for Alex's grandson, Gen. Billy Mitchell. (Library)

AMONG THE SMALL FARMING CENTERS which grew up outside Milwaukee was Wauwatosa, shown in an 1870 photo. The large white building was Thomas M. Riddle's store, which also served as the Milwaukee Road depot. (Library)

THE MILWAUKEE RIVER played a major role in the city's commerce as this 1872 sketch indicates. Shoppers stood on a boardwalk along the west bank to dicker with merchants for produce fresh off the boat. (Library)

Athens on the Kinnickinnic

BY 1880, MILWAUKEE'S POPULATION had passed the 100,000 mark and was increasing with every immigrant boat that docked. The city was a leading producer of such products as flour, leather, meat and, it goes without saying, beer. By then, it had its own wealthy aristocracy. They lived in mansions along the lake or on Grand Avenue a few blocks west of the downtown.

In politics, an organization of Civil War veterans called the Grand Army of the Republic had become a major force. For thirty years or more, anyone who aspired to high office in Milwaukee or the state was handicapped unless he had been at least a colonel. It also helped get votes if he had been wounded.

Lucius Fairchild, first of the Civil War colonels to be elected governor of Wisconsin, had lost an arm at Gettysburg. Jeremiah H. "Uncle Jerry" Rusk hadn't been lucky enough to undergo a wartime amputation but he made up for it by traveling around with an honor guard of fifteen veterans, each of whom had lost either an arm or a leg in battle.

Uncle Jerry was in office in the spring of 1886 when fourteen thousand Milwaukee workmen went on strike to demand an eight-hour day. The situation was considered so serious that the saloons were closed, an action not taken lightly in Milwaukee. Even this desperate measure failed to discourage the strikers. Rusk called out seventeen companies of militia.

On May 4, the day of the Haymarket riot in Chicago, the militiamen fired into a crowd of strikers outside the Illinois Steel Company plant in what was then the suburb of Bay View. Four of the men were killed, as was a boy who was filling the role of innocent bystander. That broke the back of the labor protest, particularly after the governor followed up the gunfire with an announcement that he would protect lives and property if he had to shoot down every striker who broke the law. Many union men felt that the militia had acted hastily. But most of Rusk's constituents considered him a hero. Mer-

A PASSENGER STEAMER, the *Sheboygan*, heads downriver past Michigan Street in this drawing made in the 1880s. Across the Milwaukee is the Mitchell Building, built in 1875 by Alexander Mitchell. Just beyond it is the Chamber of Commerce (Mackie) Building, where wheat speculators made and lost fortunes in a cavernous room called the Pit. (Library)

[34]

chant T. A. Chapman decided against running for the governorship, believing that the incumbent was now unbeatable. Uncle Jerry, a former saloonkeeper in Bad Axe County, was modest about his role.

"I seen my duty," he explained, "and I done it."

Riots, a lynching, and saloon brawls based on hard feelings between ethnic groups were a part of Milwaukee's history in the latter half of the nineteenth century, but it should not be supposed that such events were typical. Then as later, life generally went along pleasantly enough. If the working day was long, it had its compensations—the custom of sending a bucket boy out for beer, for example. If there was considerable poverty, there was also considerable affluence. Mansions went up along the lake shore and in West Side Germanic neighborhoods, some of them built by men who had arrived a decade or two before with hardly a *pfennig* in their pockets. With no income taxes to pay and a plentiful supply of inexpensive servants off the immigrant boats, the rich could live on a scale their grandchildren would envy. Even families where the breadwinner tried to make ends meet on a dollar a day had a chance for inexpensive recreation at beer gardens and parks established by the breweries. The best German theater west of New York was flourishing in Milwaukee—first at the *Stadt-Theater* on Third Street, then at a theater named for its builder, Capt. Fred Pabst. There were singing societies, shooting clubs, Turnvereins. There were private parks along the Milwaukee and fishing spots on the other two rivers, the Menomonee and the Kinnickinnic.

THE MILWAUKEE RIVER had been dredged by 1883, when this sketch was made, to permit large ships to go upstream nearly to North Avenue. The harbor entrance had been moved, and two long piers extended from it into Lake Michigan. At the end of the northern pier was a lighthouse, woth a Coast Guard life saving station behind it. The towered building in the right center is the second County Courthouse, built in 1869. (Library)

[35]

THE MENOMONEE RIVER had been dredged and straightened to provide access for lake shipping to an industrial complex. But in the settlement called Piggsville, just south of where the Wisconsin Avenue viaduct was later built, the Menomonee was a pleasant rural stream in 1884. Even when he went fishing, a properly dressed gentleman wore a derby. (Library)

Local politics was lively. Candidates wooed voters by handing out free drinks or organizing torchlight parades. For the price of a nickel beer, a man could eat heartily in the saloons. And Milwaukee was growing into a favorite destination for tourists, particularly those from Chicago who rode north on lake steamers to sample the wares offered in what was now a wide open town. Gambling houses flourished. There was plenty of good eating and hearty drinking. And there was River Street, a district that grew up around City Hall and took its name from its principal thoroughfare, which had been built atop a filled-in lagoon.

The name of the street has since been changed to Edison. In 1911, with Socialist reformers in office, the red light district disappeared after houses presided over by such madames as Kitty Williams were padlocked. The heyday of River Street was during the free and easy administration of Mayor David "All-the-Time Rosy" Rose, an amiable rapscallion who won the first of his five terms in 1898. But the district's antecedents went back to the city's early days. It was bragged about as a major tourist attraction, with visitors supplied with a printed guide to its main attractions.

The last twenty years of the nineteenth century was Milwaukee's most Germanic period, with English a minority language in some parts of town. German was taught in public as well as parochial schools from the first grade on. A parent who wanted his child to skip such classes had to get special permission. The Germans also had their own schools where all the instruction was in the language of Goethe. The German-English Academy operated by Peter Engelmann was the best known. His countrymen had their own shopping street. A non-German's money was accepted on North Third but if he spoke only English he might have trouble communicating with the clerks.

Fancy carriages with uniformed drivers and footmen pulled up at such stores as Usinger's, which made and sold sausage, and Steinmeyer's, which sold almost everything

BEFORE 1890, when the electric streetcar was introduced in Milwaukee, public transportation was based on horses or mules. The lads in the foreground of this 1880 photo of Wisconsin Street east of Jackson could travel as fast on foot as the trolleys. (Co. Hist. So.)

[37]

TRADERS ARE CHECKING samples of wheat on the floor of the Pit. Among leading speculators was a former Michigan lumberman, Angus Smith, whose motto was: "Pour out money like water rather than yield." Following this axiom, he once dropped a million dollars on a single deal. For several years, Milwaukee exported more wheat than any other port in the world. (Co. Hist. Soc.)

edible. While the lady of the house was shopping, her husband could stroll a few doors south to the Republican House, where Mrs. Charles F. Kletzsch, wife of the proprietor, presided over the kitchen. If it was meal time—and it was usually meal time in Milwaukee in those days—the newcomer might qualify for a place at the *Stammtisch*. A Stammtisch, as every good Milwaukeean knew, was a table set aside for faithful patrons where they could get together for talk and some serious eating. No one left hungry from Ma Kletzsch's restaurant, known as the Nürnberger Bratwurst-Gloecklein. The favorite dish at breakfast was sirloin steak with fried potatoes. This gave a man strength to last until noon and the fifty-cent lunch: Soup, fish, roast beef, poultry, a huge slab of pie, a bowl of nuts, and a helping of fruit, washed down with beer from foaming steins.

Women were not welcome at a Stammtisch. But they did not go hungry in nineteenth century Milwaukee. Novelist Edna Ferber, who spent her writing apprenticeship as a *Milwaukee Journal* reporter, described their typical diet:

"There were acres of cakes and kuchens. Practically every edible thing in Milwaukee was filled or ornamented with whipped cream. They put cream in the marinated herring, cream in the sauerkraut, in the soup. Their figures were frightful."

As an industrial city in need of a plentiful supply of workers, Milwaukee was still getting its full share of immigrants, not only from Germany but from other parts of Europe. By the late nineteenth century, the Irish had fallen to third place among local ethnic groups, being outnumbered not only by Germans but by newcomers from Poland.

[38]

MALE MEMBERS of the country club set were experimenting with a newfangled sport called golf. But the ladies preferred something more genteel, such as a rousing game of croquet on the front lawn. (Library)

The first Pole, Michael Skupniewicz, arrived in 1846, and seventeen years later there were enough of his countrymen living on the South Side to start the city's first Polish parish, Saint Stanislaus, later to build a church whose golden domes are a local landmark. The colony grew rapidly after the Civil War.

Lesser numbers of Bohemians, British, Dutch, Austrians, and Norwegians, in that order, also migrated to Milwaukee, along with a variety of other nationalities, notably Italians, Czechs, and Slovaks. Neighborhoods changed. Italians replaced the Irish in the Third Ward after a disastrous fire swept through the area in 1892 and left two thousand people temporarily homeless. Jewish immigrants took over an old German neighborhood on the north side, later to be replaced by blacks. The South Side, once mainly German, became largely Polish.

But the city's flavor remained predominately Teutonic in the 1880s and 1890s, even though a variety of other languages—including the Milwaukee version of English—were heard increasingly often on its streets. German residents were divided among themselves on religious, political, and economic grounds, but they were united in viewing Milwaukee as a New World Munich where the virtues of thrift, cleanliness, efficiency, and lager beer had been successfully transplanted to a Wisconsin environment. Their influence can best be illustrated by what happened when the state legislature passed the Bennett Law in 1889.

Many Wisconsin residents had begun to feel that it would be a good idea if all the state's children went to school, at least until they were old enough to quit loafing and go to work. Legislators bowed to public opinion. They decreed that every child between the ages of seven and fourteen must attend school sixty days a year.

It was not until the bill was signed by Governor William Dempster Hoard, latest in that long succession of Republicans who held office after the Civil War, that a more controversial provision of the law was revealed to the public by a belatedly alert reporter. The Bennett Law not only made education compulsory for the first time but required every school in the state to teach reading, writing, arithmetic and American history in the language spoken by Queen Victoria, not the tongue used by Otto von Bismarck.

THIS YOUNG MAN has just ridden his "bone crusher wheel" from Evanston, Illinois, to Milwaukee, a considerable feat on such a vehicle over rutted dirt roads. Note the wooden sidewalk. (Library)

A BLACKSMITH was an essential part of the urban as well as rural work force in 1880. As an increasing number of Milwaukee's streets were paved with cedar blocks, cobblestones or brick, horses could no longer go unshod. (Library)

THE MILWAUKEE CEMENT WORKS' a major industry of the 1880s, got raw material from a limestone quarry north of where Capitol Drive is now located, on the west side of the river. These men used their picks and shovels so industriously that the site later was called the Blue Hole. (Library)

Not even a ban against *sauerbraten* or *wiener schnitzel* could have caused such an uproar as broke out when this insult to the German language became known. Republican legislators hastened to explain that they'd voted for the bill without understanding it and as soon as they were voted back into office they would straighten out the situation. But there could be no acceptable excuse for the revolutionary notion that children in German districts must learn English. The Civil War colonels and the party that had so long dominated Wisconsin politics were doomed to defeat.

Differences among Wisconsin Germans were forgotten. For once, Catholics and Lutherans were of one mind. From the most junior clerk at Rich & Silber's Store to such dignitaries as Baron Ewald Alfred Arthur Frederick William "Fritz" von Cotzhausen, the railway attorney who owned the Metropolitan Block then being built at Third and State, opinion was unanimous that the Republicans must be punished. Pomeranians and Bavarians, Prussians, and Hessians, all were agreed. Not since the home team had won the Franco-Prussian War, setting off one of the wildest celebrations in Milwaukee history, had there been such a coming together of Teutonic opinion.

THE NEWALL HOUSE was built in 1857 on the northeast corner of Michigan and Broadway by Daniel Newhall. He had made his first killing as a wheat speculator when the Irish potato famine enabled him to sell $300 worth of grain for $10,000. By the time he was thirty-five years old, he was America's largest wheat dealer, owning his own fleet of freighters. He made and lost several fortunes before retiring in 1874 to a Waukesha County farm. By then, his hotel was a notorious firetrap. At the left of the hotel is Albany Hall, a favorite place for meetings and other civic functions. The hall burned down in 1862, twenty-one years before the hotel. (Library)

THE NEWHALL HOUSE burned early on the morning of January 10, 1883, with the loss of at least seventy-one lives. Some of the forty maids who lived on the sixth floor leaped into firemen's nets that were too rotten to hold them. An artist for *Frank Leslie's Illustrated Weekly* made this sketch shortly after the fire. (Library)

AMONG THOSE RESCUED from the Newhall House were Mr. and Mrs. Charles Stratton. Better known as General Tom Thumb, Stratton had been made into a twenty-five-inch celebrity by P. T. Barnum. Pres. Abe Lincoln had been among the guests at Stratton's marriage to an equally short schoolteacher at the White House during the Civil War. When the Newhall caught fire, a muscular fireman tucked the general under one arm and carried him to safety. (Co. Hist. Soc.)

[42]

FORTY-THREE of the Newhall fire's victims were too burned to be recognizable, and their religious preferences were unknown. Milwaukee solved the problem by holding two funerals for them, a mass at Saint John's Cathedral and a Protestant service at the Exposition Hall on the present site of the Milwaukee Auditorium. Nothing was left of the hotel but a few charred timbers and a heap of ashes, but spectators lined the sidewalk across the street to look at the ruins. (Library)

Delighted by their luck, the Democrats decided to nominate a Yankee, George W. Peck, as their candidate. German votes were in the bag now, so they might as well pick up additional votes from admirers of Peck's wit. As the editor of a humorous weekly newspaper, published in Milwaukee but sold nationally, and as the author of a best seller, *Peck's Bad Boy,* he was widely known. So Peck, was given a little practice as a politician by being elected mayor. Then, a few months later, he won the governorship in balloting that swept most Republicans out of office, among them a young Madison congressman, Robert M. La Follette, Sr., later to make a considerable name for himself.

Needless to say, the Bennett Law was promptly repealed. The right of a child to learn his lessons in German was restored. The heritage of Milwaukee's predominant ethnic strain had been upheld.

That was the highwater mark of German influence. Within thirty years, with the divisions and divided loyalties created in Milwaukee by World War I, the day came when sauerkraut was temporarily renamed Liberty cabbage and the Deutscher Club, which occupied Alex Mitchell's old mansion, became the Wisconsin Club. The combination of Kaiser Wilhelm and the arrival of Prohibition shortly after the war ended the old days forever.

But such traumas were a generation away in the 1880s and the Gay Nineties. Then the beer garden flourished, the Stammtisch groaned with food, the whipped cream was piled high on the kuchen. And *gemütlichkeit* held sway in a city settled by Yankees but now proudly calling itself Munich-on-the-Milwaukee, the German Athens of the New World.

[43]

BY THE LATE 1880s, such bustling intersections as the corner of Grand and West Water (now Wisconsin and Plankinton) were illuminated by electric lights, such as the handsome model shown here. The trolleys were still horsedrawn. (Marine)

FOURTEEN THOUSAND MILWAUKEEANS went on strike for the eight-hour day in 1886, and seventeen militia companies were called out. These men were guarding the Reliance Iron Works, a predecessor of the Allis-Chalmers Manufacturing Company. At another factory, the Illinois Steel Company plant, soldiers fired into a crowd of strikers. Four workmen and a boy were killed. (Journal)

EVERYONE IS TRYING to look casual for the camera in this saloon at the northeast corner of Eighth and Burleigh. The Milwaukee male ordinarily found such places an impregnable refuge from the Milwaukee female, but on this special occasion a wife and daughter have been allowed inside to pose for the picture. The wind-up phonograph at left, complete with horn, must be one of the earliest examples of the tavern jukebox. (Co. Hist. Soc.)

THESE TEMPORARILY SOBER Milwaukeeans knew a bargain when they saw one. Even in the 1880s, two beers for a nickel was not customary. (Pabst)

THAT'S ADOLPH MEINECKE, JR., on the bicycle at a family picnic. Portable lawn furniture had yet to be invented, so porch chairs were brought along. A hammock strung between two trees was even more comfortable. (Library)

FRED USINGER, SR., (fourth from right) had arrived in Milwaukee with $400 and a pocketful of sausage recipes. He lived above his market and peddled his homemade *wurst* to saloonkeepers who took pride in their free lunches. The sausage works he began in 1880 soon prospered to the point where he could afford a fine house on West Highland as well as this summer place at Donges Bay. Fred, Jr., is in the pony cart. (Usinger)

THE SHARP ANGLE required to bridge the river because of Kilbourn's refusal to have his settlement's streets match those of the East Side is indicated in this view of what is now called Wisconsin Avenue. The camera looks west. (Marine)

THE BUILDING in the center served as Milwaukee's city hall until a few years before the present one was built on the site in 1895. The earlier version was constructed in 1852 as a place for farmers and merchants to sell produce. The city took it over nine years later, replacing ground floor stalls with offices and ousting the German theatrical company which occupied the second story. (Marine)

[46]

WHEN THESE SUNDAY STROLLERS got their pictures taken in Juneau Park, Lake Michigan began just beyond the North Western Road's right-of-way. The park was later extended a considerable distance east on land built out into the lake. (Library)

CAPT. FRED PABST was forty-eight years old when he posed for this photo in 1888, the year before his father-in-law's brewery was renamed in his honor. Two years later, it was the nation's largest. (Pabst)

MASON STREET was Milwaukee's Newspaper Row in the 1880s. Even the most impressive building in the block, Adam Roth's Quiet House, had a connection with the press. Roth's free lunches kept $15-a-week reporters from having to waste money on food, and the Milwaukee Press Club was located on the third floor, connected by means of a dumb waiter to the bar. Next to Roth's was the *Seebote,* a German daily, separated from the *Milwaukee Journal* by Falk's Saloon. Three of the four other dailies were nearby. (Co. Hist. Soc.)

CIRCUSES, many of them originating in Wisconsin, were a favorite amusement. This 1885 parade is turning onto West Water (Plankinton) from Grand Avenue. (Library)

MILWAUKEE'S SECOND COURTHOUSE was built in 1869 on the site of the original one, with some city offices also located there until 1895. That's Saint John's Cathedral at the right. (Library)

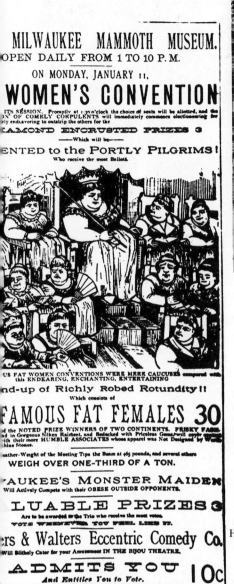
CALORIE COUNTING had not yet become a favorite sport in the Gay Nineties, particularly in Milwaukee. Excess poundage was looked on as amusing, as evidenced by this advertisement for a Fat Women's Convention. (Co. Hist. Soc.)

[49]

THE NEW CITY HALL cost $1,016,935.07, including such added equipment as this ten-ton bell for its 393-foot tower. Henry and George Campbell posed with "Old Sol" before the bell was hauled into place in 1895. Until 1922, when East Siders' complaints about a ringing in their ears persuaded aldermen to end the practice, "Old Sol" was sounded regularly. (Co. Hist. Soc.)

MILWAUKEEANS CLAIM their city has only two seasons—"winter and tough sledding." Actually, of course, the snow always melts at last, and the summers and falls are usually pleasant. The sledding was good on this Sunday of a century or so ago. Everyone who owned a sleigh was ready to take advantage of this nineteenth century version of snowmobiling. (Library)

WINTER PROVIDED commercial opportunities as well as recreation. Ice was cut on inland lakes and stored in sawdust for use in warm weather. Before mechanical refrigeration became available, easy access to ice for cooling beer was one reason for Milwaukee's leadership in brewing. (Library)

SKATING on the Milwaukee River was another favorite winter sport. These family groups are being watched by spectators on the Locust Street bridge. (Library)

WISCONSIN STREET and its westward extension, Grand Avenue, by the 1880s had long since replaced Water Street as the city's principal thoroughfare. Cream-colored brick from clay found along the Menomonee Valley was used for many buildings. An exception was the Iron Block, which can be identified by a sign advertising coal. This four-story building, which still survives, has an outer metal facade that was brought by ship from an Eastern foundry. (Marine)

HENRY J. WEHR'S Lager Beer Hall and Callahan's Billard Hall on Grand Avenue were favorite hangouts for the sporting set. Across the street, Gimbels had recently been opened by sons of a Vincennes (Indiana) merchant, Adam Gimbel. The family's expansion to Milwaukee was the start of a national department store chain. (Marine)

BETWEEN WEHR'S SALOON and the river on the west side was Pollworth's Home Restaurant, established in 1846, the year Milwaukee became a city. In this 1880 photo, the men posed on the wooden sidewalk while the women employes had to stand on the roof. The menu and most of the conversation in Pollworth's was German. (Co. Hist. Soc.)

AFTER A HEAVY SNOW, the best place to walk was between the trolley tracks, which were kept relatively clear. This photo was taken on Chestnut Street (Juneau Avenue), west of Sixth Street. (Co. Hist. Soc.)

PICTURES OF PRETTY GIRLS were recognized as a means of selling a product even in the Victorian era. Milwaukee breweries, once confined to neighborhood trade, were now competing vigorously in the national market. (Library and Co. Hist. Soc.)

JAKE NUNNEMACHER, a distiller turned investor, built his Grand Opera House across from the old city hall. Several years after this 1885 photo, Capt. Fred Pabst bought the building as a new home for a German stock company. (Library)

[54]

· THE SCHLITZ PALM GARDEN, located on the east side of Third Street south of Wisconsin Avenue, was Milwaukee's best known restaurant until it closed with the advent of Prohibition and became, for a time, a movie theater. In this photo it has been converted temporarily into a banquet hall. (Schlitz)

THE PRINCIPAL RECREATION at open-air beer gardens in the 1890s was eating heartily and lifting a few steins of the sponsor's product. Unlike the saloons, these places catered to family groups. (Co. Hist. Soc.)

GEMÜLTICHKEIT, a German word often used to describe Milwaukee's special ambience, was the order of the day when such good fellows as these got together. (Co. Hist. Soc.)

THE FIRST passenger-carrying wheel built by George W. Ferris caused great excitement at the Columbian Exposition in Chicago in 1893. Pabst's Whitefish Bay Resort installed this smaller version later that year. Awnings over the cars advertised local merchants. (Library)

THIS PHOTO was taken from the top of the Ferris wheel at Pabst's Whitefish Bay Resort, one of several private parks maintained by Milwaukee breweries. It could be reached either by rail or by lake steamers. By the time a ship's passenger had climbed those zigzag paths up the bluff, he was ready for a beer. And Pabst, you may be sure, was ready to sell him one. (Library)

THE MILWAUKEE AND WHITEFISH BAY Railway carried between 1888 and 1898 recreation seekers and a few commuters between the city and the rural village a few miles to the north. It was called "the dummy line." According to legend, the full-sized model of a horse was once mounted on a flatcar ahead of the locomotive to persuade skittish horses that the train was friendly. (Library)

THIS IS THE BUESTRIN PATENT Fire Escape, invented in the early 1870s for the Milwaukee Fire Department by Henry Buestrin, a contractor who later supervised erection of the Exposition Building. The ladder weighed more than seven thousand pounds and required three minutes to raise to its full height of ninety-five feet. It was so ungainly and awkward that it apparently was never used at an actual fire. But it impressed the onlookers at firefighters' demonstrations, such as this one outside the Central Engine House on Broadway. (Co. Hist. Soc.)

VALENTIN BLATZ, who took over Braun's Brewery in the early 1850s after marrying the founder's widow, was the first to put beer in bottles in 1875. His rivals followed suit. This not only opened up new markets for the product but gave work to women in bottling plants like this one. (Co. Hist Soc.)

Saturday, Nov. 9, 1895, at 8 P. M.

GRAND PERFORMANCE and
DEDICATION OF THE NEW THEATER

PROGRAMME:

Pabst Theater March ....Christ. Bach...... ....Grand Orchestra
Prologue...............................Written by Julius Gugler.........Recited by Ferd. Welb
Intermezzo from Cavalleria Rusticana.. ....Mascagni
        Grand Orchestra, accompanied by Organ
Debut of Flora Glasel...From the Court Theater at Detmold
        Her First Appearance in Milwaukee

"Zwei Wappen" ═══════Farce in Four Acts,
═══════By Blumenthal and Kadelburg.
Success of the Season in German Theaters of Europe.

SEATS—Box Seats, $1.50 to $1.00.   Dress Circle, $1.00.   Parquet, $1.00.   Balcony
reserved, 75c.   Balcony Circle, reserved, 50c.   Gallery, 25c.
Sale of Seats commences Tuesday, Nov. 5, at 9 a. m., in Oscar Kropf's Drug Store, on the East
Water Street side of the Pabst Theater Building.
Subscribers who desire to reserve their seats for the Opening Performance are hereby notified
to send their orders not later than Monday evening.

SUNDAY, NOVEMBER 10, 1895

SCHILLER'S BIRTHDAY
POPULAR PRICES!   POPULAR PRICES!

First Appearance of Miss ELISE WOLFF, from the Stadt Theater of Stettin

"Kabale und Liebe"

Tragedy in Five Acts, by Fr. v. Schiller.

SEATS—Dress Circle, 75c and 50c.   Parquet, 75c.   Balcony, 50c.   Balcony Circle,
35c.   Gallery, 25c.
Sale of Seats commences Tuesday, Nov. 5, in Oscar Kropf's Drug Store, on the East Water
street Side of the Pabst Theater Building

NOT LONG after Capt. Fred Pabst bought Nunnemacher's Grand Opera House, it burned down. The news was sent to the brewer in Europe, where he was vacationing. Back came a cable: "Build another one." And so the Pabst Theater opened in 1895 on the eve of Schiller's birthday, with a German stock company presenting the finest theatrical fare west of Munich. (Pabst)

[58]

AMATEUR THEATRICALS were a favorite pastime in Milwaukee society. In the picture below of the cast of some forgotten drama, Grant Fitch is the second from the right in the middle row. He later became a bank president. That's Gen. Charles King *(right)*, an Indian fighter turned Milwaukee novelist, who's making eyes at Ida Fitch in *The Mikado*. King's father, Rufus, was Milwaukee's first school superintendent, editor of the *Sentinel*, and a Civil War general. (Marine)

THE TELEPHONE reached Milwaukee in 1878, and by year's end there were fifteen subscribers. Operators like these were not spoiled by luxurious surroundings in the 1880s. At night, business was so slow that Fannie Crawford was the only operator on duty. When an interesting police call came through, she'd ring her friends on the newspapers and tip them off. On dull nights, they'd return the favor by calling her now and then so she wouldn't fall asleep. (Co. Hist. Soc.)

THE CHARLES PIETSCH FAMILY poses in front of the boyhood home of Ehrich Weiss, better known as Harry Houdini, not long after the escape artist made his first getaway—he ran away from this house on West Highland Avenue when he was twelve to join a Chicago dime museum in the early 1880s. Born either in Appleton, Wisconsin, or Hungary, depending on which biographer you believe, Houdini was a bootblack in Milwaukee and sold the first issue of the *Daily Journal* in 1882. After he became a celebrity, his old employer hired him for a promotion stunt. Dangling headfirst from the upper floor of the *Journal* building on Fourth near Wells, his arms and legs bound, he escaped as usual. (Co. Hist. Soc.)

[59]

MILWAUKEE bought its first steamer for the fire department in 1861 at a time when its aldermen had put so much tax money into mostly worthless railroad bonds that the city was nearly bankrupt. The mayor had to guarantee payment out of his own funds before the steamer was delivered. These later models are fighting a fire at the Middleton Manufacturing Company on North Broadway. (Library)

GROCERY SHOPPING was done in stores like Meldman's. The kids came along to help carry the provisions, hoping there'd be a penny or two to spare for the candy counter. (Library)

COMMISSION ROW, which successfully fought off the latest of numerous attempts to legislate it out of existence in 1975, looked like this in the days when horsepower came with four legs and a patient disposition. (Co. Hist. Soc.)

A MEMORIAL to Henry Bergh, founder of the American Society for the Prevention of Cruelty to Animals, was dedicated at this ceremony in 1891. The speaker was Gov. George Peck, a Milwaukee literary humorist who got elected because the Republicans passed a law making English compulsory in Wisconsin schools, offending those who wanted their children taught in German. The old city hall at left was torn down two years later. (Library)

THE FIRST ELECTRIC TROLLEYS began operating in 1890 and gradually drove the horsecars out of business. Streetcars like this one, pictured in 1896 with a crew of workers at the car barn, had canvas sides which could be rolled up in warm weather. (Library)

THE WATERING TROUGH at the base of the Bergh statue was used until 1941, when it was replaced with a flower bed, horses having grown scarce by then. The cafe next to the Pabst was a favorite with politicians, newsmen, and other Milwaukeeans who appreciated fattening food and the kind of leisurely atmosphere which encouraged loafing. Across the street was the Blatz Hotel. (Co. Hist. Soc.)

A *Sentinel* EDITORIAL warned that electricity was less safe than horses or mules. Sure enough, on February 4, 1895, a Milwaukee Street Railway car plunged through an open drawbridge at Kinnickinnic Avenue, killing three passengers. The trolley failed to respond to a signal showing the bridge was opening. A horse would have had better sense. (Library)

ELECTRIC INTERURBAN LINES fanned out to neighboring communities, giving Milwaukee its first crop of commuters from the suburbs. This car of the South Milwaukee line was crossing the river when the Water Street bridge was hit by a steamer, the *Kearsarge*. Car and bridge were damaged but all twelve persons aboard the interurban escaped serious injury. (Library)

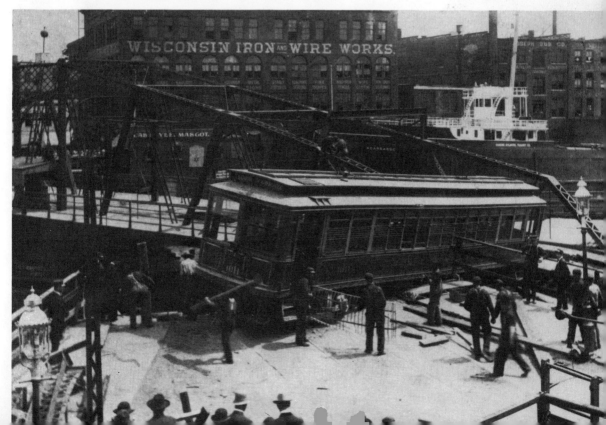

MILWAUKEE'S EAST SIDE in 1898, three years after completion of the new city hall: The tower to the extreme right is Saint John's Cathedral. At its left is the courthouse.

EUROPEANS COMPLAINED that nineteenth-century American cities were untidy. But not in Milwaukee, where Old-Country customs encouraged clean streets. This was how it was done in the days when the horse not only contributed to the problem but helped solve it. (Library)

ANOTHER MUNICIPAL HOUSEKEEPING DEVICE was the Kindling Machinery Company's "Squeegee," said to be the only machine in the world that could sprinkle, wash, and scrub a street in a single operation. (Library)

IN THE DEPARTMENT'S early years, a Milwaukee policeman could wear any sort of uniform he chose to buy as long as it was blue. But now Chief John "Czar" Janssen was in charge, and everyone had to dress alike. Until 1888, when Janssen took over. City Hall controlled the cops. Nobody controlled Janssen, as Emil Seidel learned some years later when he tried to fire him. "Go to hell," the chief told the mayor, and kept right on running the department. (Library)

CHICAGO PROMOTERS hoped to pipe spring water from Waukesha, than a nationally known health spa west of Milwaukee, to the Columbian Exposition in 1893. A local posse ran the invaders out of town. To make sure the pipe-laying crew didn't come back, this special train carried a delegation to Madison to persuade legislators not to grant the Chicagoans a franchise. (Wauk. C. of C.)

THREE OF MILWAUKEE's four National Guard regiments went into federal service in 1898 at Camp Harvey on the State Fair Grounds. Recruiting was brisk at the Broadway Armory, even though some hard-nosed sergeants wouldn't accept any Milwaukeeans who couldn't speak English. Before heading south to fight the Spaniards and free Cuba, these soldiers had time for a final stein of beer. (Pabst)

CHARLES ABRESCH, who arrived in Milwaukee from Germany in 1868, established a carriage works at Fourth and Poplar (now McKinley). Some years after this photo was taken, Abresch's establishment changed with the times by becoming a garage. (Library)

MILWAUKEE'S STREETS were still mostly unpaved in 1889, when this picture was taken at Juneau and Third, looking east. Life moved at the leisurely pace set by a team of horses. (Library)

THESE MILWAUKEE MEN about town are about to leave for a clambake in a rented carriage. (Library)

WHEN THE PASSENGERS included a band, bagpipers, and a kilted drum major, an even larger carriage was necessary. Luckily, the livery stable was equal to the challenge. (Library)

GIRLS ATTENDING the summer Vacation School had their own notions of fun, watching a dignified leader drinking from a bucket. (Library)

[68]

NUDE BATHING was permitted in Lake
Michigan in 1899, but only if the bathers
were small boys and no feminine eyes
were around. (Library)

THE SCHOENLEBER, Vilter, and Meiners families joined for this picnic on the Meiners' farm in
Waukesha County, a pleasant summer's drive west of the city. The group brought along its own mu-
sicmakers. (Library)

THE MILWAUKEE ACADEMY, whose faculty and students are shown in this 1895 photo, was one of several private schools for children of the well-to-do. (Library)

DAVID ROSE (second from left) was elected to the first of his five terms as mayor in 1898 as a reform candidate, but his administration was marked by numerous scandals, and he presided over a wide-open town. Bordellos and gambling houses were good for business, he said, because they attracted conventions and visitors from Chicago. (Co. Hist. Soc.)

Socialism, the Kaiser, and No More Free Lunch

MILWAUKEE'S FIRST TWO DECADES of the twentieth century marked the rise and decline of the Socialist Party and the agonizing split in loyalties that took place in America's most Germanic city during World War I. The Social Democrats had put their first two aldermen in office in 1876, but it was not until 1910 that the party elected a mayor, Emil Seidel, and won control of the Common Council. Municipal corruption under Dave Rose was more responsible than ideology for the Socialists' success.

Victor Berger, an Austrian who had been a cowpuncher before becoming editor of the *Milwaukee Leader,* was elected to Congress. The Socialists also captured control of the county government and became an important minority in the Legislature, voting with La Follette Progressives to pass precedent-setting social legislation. In Milwaukee, River Street was closed down, honesty was restored to City Hall, and other reforms were discussed. But Democrats and Republicans joined to oust Seidel in 1912, and the Socialists never again matched their 1910 success, although four years later Dan Hoan won the mayor's job and held onto it until 1940.

After war began in Europe in 1914, the Socialists' predominately Germanic background and the party's pacifism complicated local politics. Many Milwaukeeans were at first openly sympathetic to Kaiser Wilhelm's cause. As late as 1916 a benefit for German and Austrian war relief at the Auditorium was a huge success. But as America moved closer to joining the Allies, divisions among Milwaukeeans widened. When the United States got into the war, the statue of Germania on the Brumder Building was hidden away, a mob forced an end to German dramas at the Pabst, and any businessman with a German name who didn't buy Liberty bonds found a placard on his door, questioning his loyalty.

Milwaukee's most Germanic period ended around the century's turn, but the war accelerated the downward trend. Then, as a final insult to the good old days, Prohibition came along. It put an end to legal brewing, open air beer gardens, and the free lunch. Despite the law, no one with a dime had to go thirsty in Milwaukee. But life was never quite the same.

THE RAG MAN, who used a pushcart or horse and wagon to make his rounds, was a familiar figure in 1900 when this picture was taken. (Library)

BETWEEN MAYOR ROSE'S fourth and fifth terms was a two-year interval when a wealthy banker's son, Sherburn M. Becker, served as Milwaukee's chief executive. Elected when he was only twenty-nine years old, Sherbie celebrated his victory by driving his red Pope-Toledo all the way to Oyster Bay, New York, with a large banner trailing behind the car reading: "Milwaukee's Boy Mayor." Pres. Teddy Roosevelt was delighted to welcome a young man who was getting so much fun out of politics. (Journal)

MAYOR BECKER ordered merchants to get rid of large clocks which cluttered sidewalks on Grand Avenue. When some refused, he led a posse including an assistant city attorney and six firemen to knock the clocks down. As the sign indicates, he was running for governor then. He not only didn't move up to the Statehouse, but in 1908 Dave Rose won back the mayor's job. (Co. Hist. Soc.)

[72]

THE MEADOW SPRINGS Distilling Company, incorporated by Leopold Wirth and two partners in 1882, had changed its name to the National Distilling Company by 1905, when this photo was taken of its office. It had branched out into making vinegar and yeast as well as Livingston Whiskey and Post Hoorn and Mistletoe Gin. When Prohibition arrived, the company changed its name to Red Star Yeast and, by concentrating on that product, survived the drought. Milwaukee once had two dozen distilleries. None reopened after liquor became legal again. (Univ. Foods)

POLISH FISHERMEN took over Jones Island near the Milwaukee River's mouth in the 1870s and established a settlement so independent that even Milwaukee policemen stayed safely away. All the men did there in the summer was fish, drink, and fight, it was said by the mainlanders, and in the winter they didn't fish. By 1910, the island had softened into a tourist attraction. Visitors rowed across the river to buy fish or visit saloons run by "Governor" Anton Kanski and "Admiral" Charles Plambeck. At the height of its glory, Jones Island had 2,200 residents, seven stores, and eleven saloons. It is now the site of Milwaukee's Milorganite works, which converts sewage into commercial fertilizer. (Library)

MILWAUKEEANS BEGAN COMPLAINING about river pollution before 1880, but in the early 1900s the Milwaukee was still clean and pleasant north of the downtown section. (Library)

A RUN on the First National Bank began when depositors learned that Frank G. Bigelow, its president, had misappropriated $1,500,000 to speculate in wheat. The 1905 crisis ended after two of the bank's leading stockholders, Charles F. Pfister and Fred Vogel, Jr., proprietors of the world's leading tannery, brought gold bullion from Chicago and paraded it through the city streets to the bank. Vogel became president, and Bigelow got ten years in a federal penitentiary. The First National later merged with the Wisconsin National Bank to become the First Wisconsin National Bank, the state's largest. (1st Wis.)

A RESIDENT of an East Side mansion whose butler had neglected to buy enough beer could put in a hurried call to Pabst, which would rush fresh supplies in this handsome carriage with its uniformed attendants. (Co. Hist. Soc.)

POOL WAS AS POPULAR in Milwaukee around the turn of the century as bowling became later. These sportsmen, shown outside a pool hall on Green Bay Avenue, called themselves "the Bloody Sixty-Four." (Library)

MUSCLEPOWER was the principal means used in putting up or tearing down buildings in 1900, but the men who were razing the old post office at Milwaukee Street and Wisconsin had rigged up an ingenious arrangement to lift a loaded wagon out of the pit. The man in the straw hat is Samuel J. Broahman. He later supervised construction of the Wells Building, an early Milwaukee version of a skyscraper. (Co. Hist. Soc.)

WHEN THE EXPOSITION BUILDING burned down during a convention of skat players, it was replaced by the Milwaukee Auditorium, shown in early stages of construction in 1908. (Co. Hist. Soc.)

THE "JAHRMARKT" on Grove Street (South Fifth) gave shopping a festive air. By 1905, when this picture was made, the neighborhood was becoming more Polish than German—but everybody in Milwaukee knew what the "Willkommen" signs meant. (Library)

HAYMARKET SQUARE, on the near north side, provided a place for farmers to sell not only horse feed but vegetables, eggs, and other produce directly to consumers. (Co. Hist. Soc.)

WHEN JOSEPH GEBHARDT hitched a steer to a cutter in 1912 and drove downtown from suburban Brookfield, the days when ox teams were common sights in Milwaukee streets had long since vanished. He wanted to show that, despite all those cars running around, the old ways had their advantages when the snow was on the ground. (Library)

EUROPEAN IMMIGRANTS brought with them the knowledge of how to convert grapes into wine, even in a climate like Wisconsin's. These vintners at the Kern vineyards on the city's north side are members of the Kern and Meinecke families.

A MILWAUKEE POLICEMAN was walking his beat in Humboldt Park about 1900 when somebody said, "Hey, you want to get in the picture with the kids?" "Don't mind if I do," says he, and here he is. (Library)

PITCHING MARBLES required serious concentration, as these boys and the spectators demonstrate. (Muni. Rec.)

TO CREATE a backyard skating rink, someone had to do a lot of work with a pump handle. Now these skaters are enjoying their reward. (Library)

UNTIL AUTOMOBILES REPLACED them as the handiest means of getting around without hitching up a horse, bicycles enjoyed their period of greatest popularity. This bike race was held on Blue Mound Road, the main highway between Milwaukee and Waukesha. (Library)

THE DEUTSCHER PRESS CLUB was begun at a time when two of every three Milwaukee newspaper readers got their news in German. By 1900, when this group posed for its picture at the Pine Lake estate of George Brumder, head of a Milwaukee-based chain of newspapers, the English-language dailies had forged ahead as the city's percentage of native Germans declined. (Library)

MILWAUKEE'S ZOO, now among the nation's top half-dozen, got its start with a single cage of monkeys at Washington Park. As part of the zoo's gradual expansion, a pool was added and supplied with seals whose antics drew big crowds *(below)*. Countess Heine, the zoo's first elephant *(left)*, arrived in 1907. The six-year-old was greeted at the depot by an organization of civic leaders known as the Elephant Marching Club. On the way to Washington Park, the group stopped at the Pabst Brewery. The countess got a bale of hay tied with blue ribbon and her escort lifted a glass or two in her honor. (Library)

EVERYONE IN THE FAMILY helped out in the Otto Gahns bakery on Second Street in 1902, so everybody was entitled to get in the picture. (Library)

CUSTOMERS had to supply their own containers for milk in 1900. Harry Jung, a driver for the Splinter Dairy Company, waits while George Janowitz pours. (Library)

WHEN the Gridley Dairy Company wagon was loaded with 100 eighty-eight-gallon cans of milk, the four-horse hitch had to pull nearly eighty tons. Gridley supplied Milwaukeeans with milk from 1897 to 1942, when it became a Bordon Company Division. (Library)

HERMAN TOSER'S, founded in 1880 to wholesale liquor, wine, and other necessities for the drinking man, managed to survive after Prohibition began by supplying medicinal alcohol to drug stores. An amazing number of Milwaukeeans found themselves in need of such first aid. (Library)

HENRY WEBER, proprietor of Weber and Stuber's, managed to maintain his dignity one afternoon in 1913 while he and the gentlemen in the back seat were pretending that the bear was driving the car. Weber's restaurant and saloon was a favorite hangout for politicians until it was closed by Prohibition. (Library)

MILWAUKEE'S FIRST AUTOMOBILE was built by Frank Toepfer, a machinist, in 1890 at the suggestion of Gottfried Schloemer, a barrelmaker. It had a top speed of ten miles an hour. Some years later, Fay L. Cusick exhibited the vehicle at fairs, billing it as the world's oldest, a claim open to considerable doubt. The car is now at the Milwaukee Museum. (Library)

AND HERE is Milwaukee's first mail truck, put in service in 1907. (Library)

AUTOS HAD BECOME more numerous than horses at the corner of Wisconsin and Jefferson by 1914. At right is an electric model, a sedate sort of car favored by dowagers. Next to the curb at the left is a typical street scene—a motorist cranking while a friend leans into the auto to manipulate the controls on the steering wheel. (Library)

THE WELLS STREET TROLLEY rattled back and forth across this bridge over the Menomonee Valley, providing the most exciting ride in town when this picture was taken in 1907. (Library)

THE MILWAUKEE CLUB, which a member jokingly described recently as an organization "for old men and their fathers," is the red brick building across from the Pfister Hotel in this 1905 photo. The club was established in 1882 with Alexander Mitchell as its first president. Mitchell's house later became the headquarters for the Wisconsin Club, the Milwaukee's chief rival for the local society trade. (Library)

GERMAN SINGING SOCIETIES such as the Manner-Chor Eichenkranz were numerous in Milwaukee before World War I. Some managed to survive the sometimes hysterical suspicion of anything German that occurred with American entry into the fighting against Kaiser Wilhelm. (Library)

THE CENTENNIAL of Oliver Hazard Perry's victory over a British fleet in Lake Erie during the War of 1812 called for a celebration in such Great Lakes cities as Milwaukee. The Wisconsin Avenue bridge was all spruced up for a parade. (Library)

EVEN SPECTATOR SPORTS could be rugged. If you wanted to see a skating race on the frozen Milwaukee, you climbed down the embankment, stood in the snow, pulled your cap over your ears and watched it. This contest was held about 1915. (Muni. Rec.)

REPLACING a bicycle's front wheel with a skate made for an exciting race, particularly on the turns. But this leg-powered early version of a snowmobile never caught on except with daredevils like these. (Muni. Rec.)

[86]

A BREWERY called Falk, Jung and Borchert had turned out 200,000 barrels a year until stopped by disastrous fires in 1889 and 1891. It was sold to a competitor, Capt. Fred Pabst. Three years later, Phillip Jung bought the Obermann Brewery and organized the Jung Brewing Company, whose employes posed for this 1901 photo. Within the next decade, Jung had risen to fifth place among Milwaukee beer makers. (Co. Hist. Soc.)

ST. PAUL AVENUE had not been paved in 1904, but there was a wooden sidewalk when these telephone linemen brought service to the neighborhood. Seven men weren't really needed on a single pole. But how else could they all get in the picture? (Co. Hist. Soc.)

THE UIHLEIN THEATER, with check rooms for bicycles on the second floor and four bars where Schlitz beer was sold, was opened in 1896. A few months later, its name was changed to the Alhambra. In 1907, when the billboard crew led by advertising agent Arthur Dunn paused for the cameraman, "The Isle of Bong Bong" was the stage show. The theater was razed in 1959. (Co. Hist. Soc.)

MALES COULD NOT GO TOPLESS at Milwaukee beaches, but such immodesty was permitted at Rohn's Swimming School on the Milwaukee River above a dam near North Avenue. It was during this period when Theda Bara, the silent screen vamp who had been Theodosia Goodman when she lived in Milwaukee, refused to appear in a one-piece bathing suit at the Alhambra, claiming such a costume was indecent. (Co. Hist. Soc.)

EVERY WEEKDAY at 6:30 a.m., drivers and their teams lined up in the Pabst Brewery yards to carry lager to a thirsty city. (Co. Hist. Soc.)

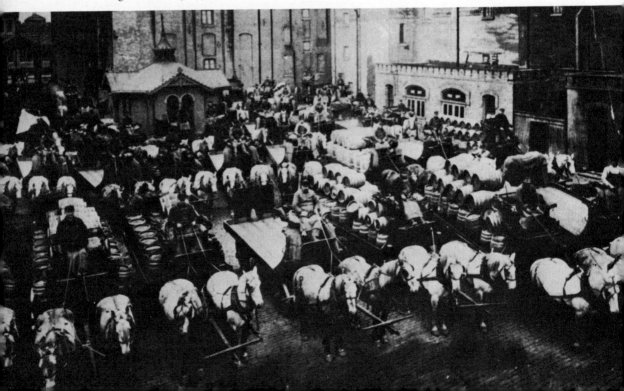

AFTER THE BEER BARRELS had left
the brewery for the saloon trade, it was
the turn of wagons like this that carried
bottled goods. Three matched pairs of
dappled grays kept the supplies moving
briskly. (Co. Hist. Soc.)

SCHWARTZ'S, one of the first stops for
Pabst's wagons, was located three blocks
east of the brewery. At most saloons, a
man was expected to stand with one foot
on the brass rail, but Schwartz provided
wooden chairs and tables. (Co. Hist. Soc.)

THERE WASN'T MUCH CALL for gasoline when this Standard Oil wagon
paused in front of William W. Douglas'
harness shop. But the firm did a thriving
business in kerosene for "coal oil" lamps
and stoves. (Library)

CAPT. CHARLES E. MOODY was skipper of the *Christopher Columbus,* the only whaleback steamboat ever to carry passengers. During a two-hour layover in Milwaukee in 1905, he sent his wife, mother, sister, and daughter along on this tally-ho excursion—they're in the middle compartment. The *Christopher Columbus* carried passengers between Milwaukee and Chicago from 1893 to 1929. In 1917 it hit a support for a steel water tank along the Milwaukee River. The tank tipped over onto the ship, killing sixteen persons. (Library)

THE S.S. VIRGINIA COACH LINE provided this sightseeing carriage for Milwaukee passengers in 1901. One reason for the popularity of the steamers from Chicago was the ease of getting married in Milwaukee. Marrying preachers sent runners to meet the ships and drum up business. The ceremonies were brief, giving newlyweds plenty of time to see the sights in romantic Milwaukee. (Co. Hist. Soc.)

THE MILWAUKEE ELECTRIC RAILWAY and Light Company, successor to a number of rival horsecar lines, was installing service facilities on South Sixth when workmen paused for a picture in 1911. By then, the company had one hundred forty miles of track for its trolleys. It also had 13,582 customers for its electric current. For some years, only homes and businesses close to a streetcar line could get electric service. (Library)

AUGUST UIHLEIN (second from left) owned the largest block of stock in the Jos. Schlitz Brewing Company, and before his death in 1911 had become Milwaukee's richest man. Alfred Uihlein (far right) outlived his six brothers and was board chairman of the family brewery when Prohibition ended in 1933. Between them is William Uihlein, who introduced the process of pure yeast culture to the brewery. (Co. Hist. Soc.)

THE HORSE might be losing out to the automobile, but military men followed their old habit of preparing for the next war by practicing the tactics of the last one. Troop A, shown at Fred Usinger's country place at Donges Bay, demonstrated its readiness for a cavalry charge. (Usinger)

THE GROWING POPULARITY of the automobile changed the city's appearance. The sightseeing bus, parked on Second just off Wisconsin, offered a tour of Milwaukee for fifty cents. Some customers were less thrilled by the sights than by a chance to ride in a vehicle not pulled by a horse. (Co. Hist. Soc.)

ANOTHER METHOD of getting around without a horse was the "motor wheel" made by Steve Briggs and Harry Stratton, shown here with the original model. The Briggs & Stratton Corporation later helped make Milwaukee a world leader in the manufacture of small engines. (Co. Hist. Soc.)

AUTOMOBILES were still mostly a rich man's toy in 1908, but an enterprising plumber, John A. Bechtel, proved that they could be useful for the working man, too. (Co. Hist. Soc.)

DURING THE PERIOD when automobiles were a novelty, motorcycles made in Milwaukee were becoming world-renowned. That's William Harley in the driver's seat. William Davidson is in the sidecar with the fish. Harley-Davidson Company grew from a backyard workshop into one of the city's major industrial plants. (Library)

A HARNESS TRACK was opened in 1908 at Washington Park by the Gentlemen's Driving Club, headed by Mayor Rose. The grandstand was erected shortly before this picture was taken in 1915. It doubled as a boathouse for the lagoon. There was a beer garden nearby where the winners could gloat and the losers could drown their disappointment. (Library)

VICTOR BERGER, shown at a polling booth with his wife, Meta, was a leading Milwaukee Socialist and the man who persuaded Eugene V. Debs, its presidential candidate, to join the party. Berger's twenty-year sentence for violation of the Espionage Act for pacifistic writings during the war was imposed by Judge Kenesaw Mountain Landis, later baseball commissioner. It was overturned by the Supreme Court and Berger went back to Congress. (Journal)

TO COUNTER SOCIALIST VICTORIES, Republicans and Democrats combined to pass a state law making city elections nonpartisan. But as this horsedrawn billboard of 1914 indicates, the major parties continued to worry. They had reason. That was the year when Socialist Dan Hoan won the mayorality, hanging onto the job for twenty-six straight years. (Co. Hist. Soc.)

BEING A LONG DISTANCE telephone operator was hard work in 1910, with a call from Milwaukee to Madison often taking an hour or more to put through, if a connection could be made at all. These young women deserved their Sunday at Waukesha Beach to wave banners and tennis rackets. (Library)

SOCIAL CENTERS provided inexpensive entertainment as well as instruction. At this 1913 dancing class at the Dover Street Center, the mysteries of the one-step were attacked with considerable earnestness, judging from the dancers' expressions. (Muni. Rec.)

SUFFRAGETTES were marching and would soon get the vote, but most girls were more concerned with domestic arts than politics. At this "housewifery class" at the Center Street Playground in 1914, the lesson involves shampooing the hair in a washbowl, a skill that would come in handy. (Muni. Rec.)

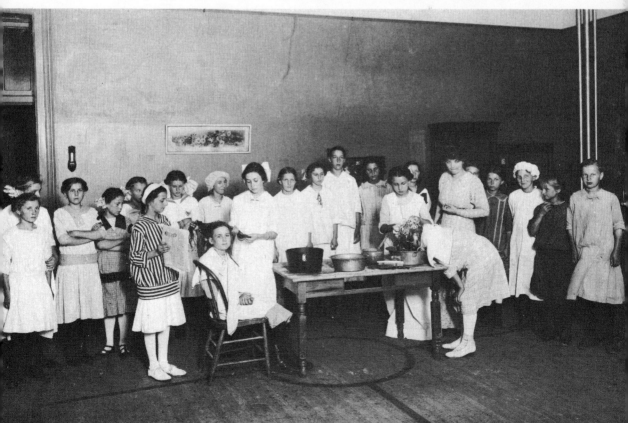

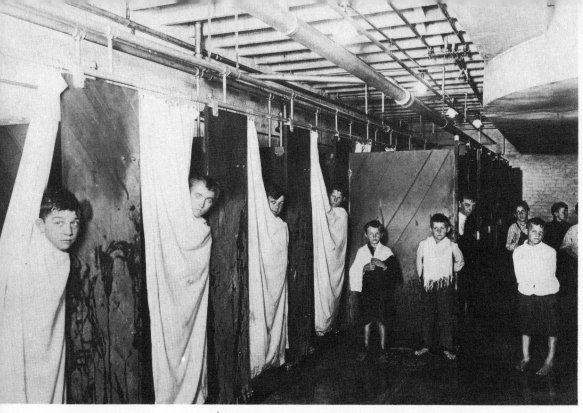

CLEANILINESS was also advocated for boys, who were not always enthusiastic. Showers at city recreation centers often were the lads' first introduction to a method of taking a bath without using the family washtub. (Muni. Rec.)

McKINLEY BEACH was crowded on this August day in 1914. Few ventured into the water, Lake Michigan being as chilly then as now. (Library)

DESPITE LONG DRESSES, the Milwaukee working girl believed in exercise. This lively volleyball game was played during a noon hour in 1913 at the Seventh Street Playground. The young women had jobs in the neighborhood. (Muni. Rec.)

KNICKERS were not special uniforms for this ball game at Lapham Park. That's how boys dressed in 1913 until the happy day when Dad said they were ready for long pants. (Muni. Rec.)

TEDDY ROOSEVELT was the nation's only living ex-president when he strode confidently out of the depot on his way to a campaign speech at the Milwaukee Auditorium in 1912. He had split with the Republican president, William Howard Taft, and was running against him on the Bull Moose ticket. Not long after this photo was made, John Schrank shot Roosevelt outside the Gilpatrick Hotel on Third south of Kilbourn. Luckily, the manuscript of his speech in Teddy's pocket was bulky enough to slow down the bullet. Roosevelt gave his talk, then went to the hospital. (Co. Hist. Soc.)

CARIBOU BILLY COOPER and his Alaskan dog team played the Lyric Theater in South Milwaukee in 1910. To drum up business and advertise Indian motorcycles, Billy gave passersby an advance peak at the act. Mud streets were still not uncommon and in South Milwaukee the horse and buggy seemed to be holding its own against competition from the horseless carriage. (Co. Hist. Soc.)

LONG BEFORE juvenile delinquency had become a major concern, it was recognized as a good idea to keep boys off the streets. This is the "quiet room" in a social center at the Fourth Street School in 1912. That school's most famous graduate, incidentally, was Morris Mabowehz's daughter, Goldie. As Mrs. Golda Meir, she served as prime minister of Israel. (Muni. Rec.)

A GENTEEL OCCUPATION for women who had to make a living was making and selling women's hats. These Milwaukeeans are enrolled in a millinery class at the Clarke Street Social Center. (Library)

ROLLING A HOOP was considered a suitable sport for girls in 1914. This hoop race was held at the Center Street playground. (Muni. Rec.)

BY 1914, THE YEAR war broke out in Europe, the saloon was under heavy attack by Prohibitionists. Brewery workers, among others, were concerned. Union members are waiting on Fourth Street to march on Wisconsin Avenue. The prediction on one sign that "moonshine takes the place of good beer" proved accurate a few years later, although buying beer never became much of a problem in Milwaukee despite the official ban. (Co. Hist. Soc.)

AMERICAN SOLDIERS had done no serious fighting since 1865 aside from the brief Spanish-American War. Such military units as the Milwaukee Hebrew Guards, pictured at the Fourth Street School, were getting ready for World War I, although they didn't know it when they posed for this photo in 1913. (Muni. Rec.)

AFTER WORLD WAR I began in Europe in 1914, life went on, for a time, much as before in Milwaukee. Residents might differ about whether the Germans or the British and French were the good guys in the conflict, but at a concert in the park the fighting still seemed very far away. (Co. Hist. Soc.)

TIMES WERE PROSPEROUS as the United States, still theoretically neutral, became the chief supplier of the Allied armies. But there continued to be a market for secondhand clothes along Third Street and West Wells, part of a section then known to the police as the Bad Lands. (Co. Hist. Soc.)

WITH AMERICAN ENTRY into the fighting, Milwaukee parades took on a wartime flavor. This one is promoting support of the American Red Cross. The children nearest the camera are from the Grant Street School. (Co. Hist. Soc.)

THIS UNIFORM became all too familiar to thousands of young Milwaukeeans. Joseph Koshak was among them. (Library)

MILWAUKEE was a favorite spot for sailors on weekend passes. Sometimes the recruits from Great Lakes Naval Training Station across the Illinois border came on more formal visits, as at this demonstration by the "boots" in Juneau Park. (Library)

SENATOR "FIGHTING BOB" LA FOLLETTE, SR. (right), who had pushed through precedent-setting social legislation as governor, opposed American entry into World War I. Enough voters agreed with him to keep him in office. His son, Robert, Jr. (left), later succeeded him as Wisconsin senator. (Library)

WELLS, FARGO & COMPANY, which helped open up the West by delivering goods and people, had its Milwaukee headquarters on Third Street near the Milwaukee Road station. In 1918, a year after this picture of employes and equipment was made, it merged with several other companies to form American Railway Express. (Library)

THE YOUNG claimed to be members of the lost generation and disillusioned, but the 1920s was an era of heroes—Babe Ruth, Jack Dempsey, Red Grange. The greatest adulation was reserved for a young Minnesotan who had attended the University of Wisconsin. After Charles A. Lindbergh flew alone from New York to Paris, he returned in triumph aboard a warship dispatched by Calvin Coolidge. When "Lucky Lindy" visited, Milwaukee gave a pretty fair imitation of Manhattan's ticker tape parade *(above)* despite a shortage of skyscrapers and, for that matter, of ticker tape. The motorcade on Wisconsin Avenue *(below)* brought out the largest crowd since the celebration of the end of World War I. Every politician in town tried to crowd into the roadster with the "Lone Eagle," and Mayor Dan Hoan was one who made it. (Library-Co. Hist. Soc.)

The Twenties

"I DON'T WANT any dry votes," Charlie Schallitz announced during the Prohibition era, just before being elected Milwaukee County sheriff. The city was among the wettest in the land. It was also one of the most law-abiding in other respects, as the Wickersham Commission appointed by President Hoover attested when the decade had ended.

Milwaukee juries refused to convict anyone serving the public's demand for beer. But the gangsterism that was notorious ninety miles to the south was generally avoided by a combination of honesty in City Hall and tough enforcement by chiefs John Janssen and Jake Laubenheimer.

"Crime on Sunday, Waupun on Monday"—that was the motto. And criminals were apt to find themselves in the state prison at Waupun even faster if their home address was Chicago.

SILENT MOVIES were threatening vaudeville as the leading form of entertainment, and Daniel Webster Hoan, the Socialist mayor, was willing to pose for a newsreel cameraman. (Library)

[106]

DARK WOOD, marble floors, and an air of dignity were the rule in places where bankers did business. This is the National Exchange Bank, which was proud of having a capital and surplus of one million dollars. (Marine)

WHEN THE L-4, a tri-motor with a wing-spread of one hundred sixty-eight feet, was built by Albert W. Lawson's company in Milwaukee, it was the world's largest airplane. Its cabin, designed for thirty-four passengers, came equipped with bunks and a shower bath. Unfortunately for Lawson and aviation, the L-4's wingtip brushed an elm as it was taking off on its first flight in 1921. The airliner was wrecked, Lawson's company went broke, and Milwaukee's dream of becoming the nation's aviation capital ended. (Co. Hist. Soc.)

MILWAUKEE'S first winter sports meet was held in 1925 at Gordon Park. It took courage for this first jumper to go off an improvised ski hill as spectators watched from the icy hillside along the river. (Muni. Rec.)

THE MILWAUKEE ICE CARNIVAL of 1926 featured skating and hockey on the river as well as skiing. (Mun. Rec.)

SOME MILWAUKEEANS preferred indoor sports. The Charleston might be the rage at the road houses on Blue Mound Road, but at the Auer Avenue School gymnasium the fox trot and waltz were preferred. (Muni. Rec.)

THE 1920s FLIVVER gave the young a new freedom of movement, making it possible to speed off at a breathtaking forty miles an hour to places that had been out of reach with a horse. (Library)

A ONE-PIECE SWIMMING SUIT for women had become respectable toward the end of decade. Betty Ludwig (left), instructor at the Center Street Natatorium, is wearing one. Milwaukee's natatoriums not only provided swimming pools but offered residents without indoor plumbing a chance to take a bath. (Muni. Rec.)

THIS HOTEL at Third and Kilbourn had been the Republikaner Haus until its name was Anglicized. In the 1920s, it was operated by Alvin Kletzsch, the University of Wisconsin's first football coach, and his brother, Herman, still remembered for setting off the loudest firecrackers in town on New Year's Eve. The American League was organized in Room 185 in 1899, with Milwaukee a charter member. (Library)

MANY BOYS helped with the family finances as soon as they were old enough to sell papers. Newsboys fought for the best corners, sometimes with adult reinforcements from the rival dailies' circulation departments. The Newsboys' Republic encouraged good citizenship and channeled youthful energy into sports instead of street brawls. (Muni. Rec.)

BEFORE WISCONSIN ROADS were marked, Walter "Brownie" Rowland, *Milwaukee Journal* sports editor and promotion man, drove around putting up signposts and sending back advice on how a motorist could get from one place to another without getting lost. This is a typical rural road of the period. (Co. His. Soc.)

BROWNIE IS BIDDING GOODBYE to his boss, Harry J. Grant, *Journal* publisher, before setting off on another daring jaunt on Wisconsin's highways. Rowland usually took along an assistant known as "the Poor Cuss" to write his column and fix tires. (Co. Hist. Soc.)

A MILWAUKEE FLIER, Lester Maitland, was welcomed home after his three-engine Fokker monoplane made the first flight from California to Hawaii. The plump fellow with the straw skimmer is Sheriff Charlie Schallitz who used to tell his reporter friends: "Write me up good or write me up bad, boys, but write me up." (Library)

A LANDING FIELD constructed on the lakefront near downtown in the 1920s was named for Lester Maitland. (Library)

OTTO BORCHERT was president of the Milwaukee Brewers, a team which dropped out of the American League in 1902 and joined the newly-organized American Association. The city didn't return to the big leagues until 1953. (Co. Hist. Soc.)

DESPITE GENERALLY PROSPEROUS times, there were troubles between management and labor, as evidenced by this picket outside a Milwaukee theater. The owner of the new 1927 Chevrolet at the curb has replaced the original equipment with a bumper of his own devising. (Library)

SUCH SANDLOT TEAMS as the Kosciuszko Reds, headed by H. L. Polewczynski, sometimes drew larger crowds than the Brewers. Their games had an unbeatable advantage: free admission. (Library)

MILWAUKEE'S FIRST BLACK RESIDENT was Joe Oliver, Solomon Juneau's cook, who voted in the first election held in 1835. But by 1929, when this popcorn party was held at the Vliet Street Playground, blacks remained a small minority in the city. Most lived in what was called Bronzeville, a near northside neighborhood that had been German, then Jewish. (Muni. Rec.)

WHEN THE MOVIES began to talk, Milwaukeeans reacted with proper enthusiasm. This crowd was waiting to see *The Cockeyed World* at the Strand. (Library)

SHANTY TOWNS, called "Hoovervilles," went up around most major cities, including Milwaukee. Not long after this 1931 photo was taken, shacks in Lincoln Park were washed away by the spring floods. (Co. Hist. Soc.)

CONSTRUCTION of a new courthouse and razing of the old one had begun before hard times struck. This bust of Solomon Juneau had presided over the county building at Cathedral Square, where pigeons were no respecters of city founders. (Co. Hist. Soc.)

THE DEPRESSION was not permitted to end the habit of holding parades. This one was for Wiley Post and Harold Gatty, who flew around the world in 1931 in eight days and fifty-one minutes in their monoplane, the *Winnie Mae*. Four years later, Post and comedian Will Rogers were killed in a plane crash in Alaska. (Library)

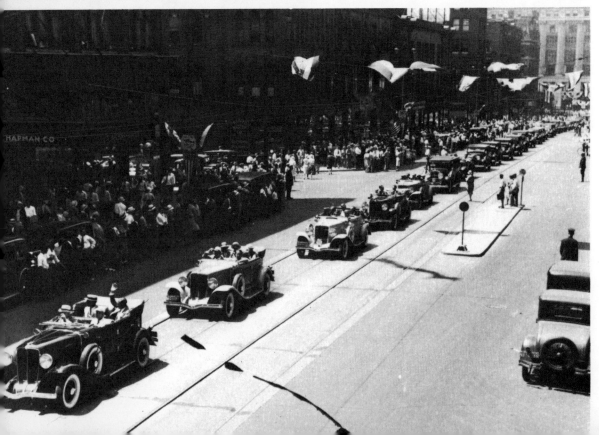

The Difficult Thirties

LOOKING BACK, it is plain that the soaring prosperity of the 1920s ended with the 1929 stock market crash. But for a while, Milwaukee had hopes that it would avoid the Depression. For months after hard times had arrived elsewhere, employment continued strong, and job hunters converged on the city. But by 1931, the backlog of factory orders was exhausted and the most serious economic crisis of the nation's history had reached the banks of the Milwaukee, the Menomonee, and the Kinnickinnic.

ONE OF THE MOST WIDELY discussed schemes for ending the hard times was originated by Dr. Francis E. Townsend (left), a California physician, who stopped in Milwaukee to seek support from Mayor Hoan. The Townsend Plan called for paying $200 a month to every retired citizen over sixty, with the money to be spent within thirty days. At its height, the Townsend movement had two and a half million members. Passage of the Social Security Act in 1935 weakened the plan's appeal. (Library)

RADICAL MOVEMENTS made some progress with the unemployed, particularly before New Deal measures began to relieve some of the worst hardships. These men listened to Communist speakers at a rally at Haymarket Square in the winter of 1930, then marched to the courthouse to demand work. A month later, fifty-one persons were arrested at the Haymarket in what was called a labor riot. (Library)

LABOR UNIONS became more militant during the troubled 1930s, using such techniques as sit-down strikes. At this demonstration, union members marched around City Hall to demand action by the city to provide more jobs. (Library)

ELECTED IN A LANDSLIDE VICTORY over Herbert Hoover, Franklin D. Roosevelt was at the height of his popularity when he stopped at the North Western Road depot in 1934. Enjoying a laugh at the president's quip are (left to right) Sen. F. Ryan Duffy, Rep. Thomas D. O'Malley, FDR, John Roosevelt, Sen. Robert M. La Follette, Jr., and Gov. Albert G. Schmedeman. (Journal)

MILWAUKEE ESTABLISHED a center where unemployed men could read, play cards, and learn such skills as shoe repairing. Such knowledge was unlikely to lead to a job, but it was useful to know how to fix the family's footwear. (Muni. Rec.)

THE COUNTY put men to work building roads, By using picks and shovels instead of machinery, a maximum number of workers could be hired. (Library)

SEN. F. RYAN DUFFY (left) engaged in mock combat with Sen. Allen Ellender of Louisiana to celebrate the end of a Congressional session. A Milwaukee Democrat, Duffy later became a federal judge. (Library)

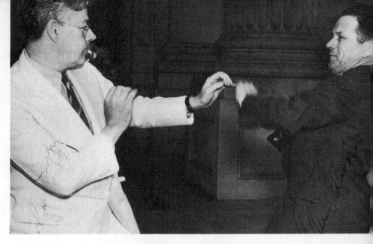

ONE WIDELY HELD THEORY in the Depression's early years was that hard times were caused by the refusal of those who had money to spend it. The First Wisconsin National Bank issued this pledge *(below)* to anyone withdrawing funds. (1st. Wis.)

ANTI - HOARDING CERTIFICATE
for the information of the United States Government

Date_____1933

I hereby certify that this withdrawal of $_____will not be hoarded but will be used promptly for

_____

_____

_____

FIRST WISCONSIN NATIONAL BANK   _____

TOWARD THE END of the Depression, Gov. Julius P. Heil stopped to inspect a bookbinding project sponsored by the WPA, one of the principal New Deal agencies to give work to the unemployed. A genial Milwaukee millionaire known as "Julius the Just," Heil lasted only one term. (Library)

THESE MEN are watching history made—that's the first case of Blatz to move out of the brewery one minute past midnight on April 7, 1933, when Congress decreed that 3.2 beer was no longer intoxicating. Milwaukee's celebration that night was much more enthusiastic than when Prohibition officially ended the following December 5th. With beer legal, eighty-five hundred brewery workers in Milwaukee got jobs. (Journal)

WITH THE RETURN OF BEER, the fine old custom of rushing the growler was revived. Bud Schroeder, a cooper's apprentice at the Blatz Brewery, is taking a load of foaming growlers to fellow workers. (Journal)

ERWIN UIHLEIN (third from left), Schlitz president, and others posed with kegs of the product the night beer became legal again. Sol Abrams, vice president of the brewery, is at the far right. (Co. Hist. Soc.)

CELEBRITIES VISITING MILWAUKEE generally found themselves being entertained in a brewery. Groucho Marx is lifting a stein with Fred Pabst, son of Capt. Fred. (Pabst)

LAURITZ MELCHIOR (center), the opera star, tackles a fishbowl of brew as his wife looks on anxiously. (Pabst)

[121]

THE COMEDY team of Chic Johnson and Ole Olsen *(below)* overwhelmed a midget named Andy Ratousheff with Milwaukee hospitality. (Pabst)

THAT'S YOUNG GUS MADER (fifth from left, front row) and his father in front of what was to become one of the city's best known German restaurants, after considerable remodeling. (Library)

[122]

IF YOU HAVE two loaves of bread, a poet once advised, sell one and buy hyacinths. The need for beauty persisted even during the great Depression. It was 1931 when the flower peddler's wagon stopped to sell its cargo of growing things. (Library)

FOR THE FIRST TIME in twenty-two years, the Milwaukee Brewers won the American Association championship in 1936. The town's heroes were loaded aboard fire trucks and hauled past their fans. (Journal)

THE DEPRESSION brought a change in women's dress styles. The flapper of the 1920s disappeared, along with the boyish look. These volleyball champs of the Walter Allen Playground show what was being worn in 1933. (Muni. Rec.)

THE AGE OF STEAM was ending for the railroads, and the Milwaukee Road station would never look quite the same after locomotives like these departed for good. (Co. Hist. Soc.)

RAILROAD FANS stood watching as the Milwaukee Road's *Hiawatha* made its first run in 1935. The train routinely covered the eighty-five miles between Milwaukee and Chicago in seventy-five minutes. An engineer made the trip in a record fifty-seven minutes in 1939. He was suspended from his job for speeding. (Library)

SIMPLY FLYING ACROSS the ocean wasn't unusual enough in 1938 to make a man a hero. He needed a gimmick. Douglas Corrigan, who had seen Lindbergh's take-off for Paris eleven years before, found one. He claimed he'd flown the Atlantic by mistake, having intended to go to California. That was amusing enough to entitle him to an enthusiastic Milwaukee welcome. He is waving to a State Fair crowd in suburban West Allis. (Library)

THE WASHINGTON PARK ZOO was an inexpensive place to spend time during the Depression. These bear dens were later torn down to make way for a freeway, with a greatly expanded new zoo built on a wooden site at the city's western edge. (Muni. Rec.)

FOR BOYS in the 1930s, when fireworks were sold freely, the Fourth of July was a highlight of the year. John Trojahn is ready to make noise. The clerk is Lillian Frenn. (Journal)

[126]

THE 1940s BEGAN with a late spring flood that sent the Milwaukee River over its banks. (Library)

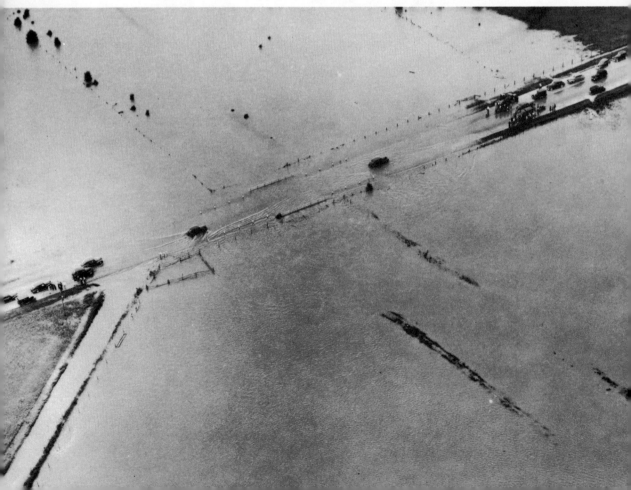

The Forties and Beyond

WORLD WAR II brought changes in Milwaukee's ethnic mix, with refugees arriving from Europe and blacks moving north to seek jobs. The economy began booming at last as factories turned out goods for the battlefronts. On weekends, the streets were crowded with servicemen, particularly the sailors who rode the North Shore electric trains from Great Lakes Naval Training Station.

AS NAZI ATROCITIES and the outbreak of war lent new impetus to migration to America, Milwaukee fulfilled its traditional role as a refuge for newcomers from Europe. This class in English and citizenship was held at Siefert Social Center in the spring of 1941. (Muni. Rec.)

SUCH DANCE HALLS as the Wisconsin Roof and George Devine's Million Dollar Ballroom were flourishing. But first youths had to learn to dance. This class was at Victor Berger Social Center. (Muni. Rec.)

SOME YOUNG WOMEN went in for modern dance, as in this program at Lincoln High School. (Muni. Rec.)

THE LAPHAM PARK ENGLISH CLASS presented this cheerful-looking chorus line. The members were from five different countries—Russia, Palestine, Denmark, Poland, and France. (Muni. Rec.)

HARVEY DEUTSCH and his albino horse, Peewee, entertained youngsters on North Twenty-seventh Street. (Muni. Rec.)

[130]   WITH AMERICA'S ENTRY into the war a few months off, veterans of World War I gathered for a final fling at the 1941 American Legion convention in Milwaukee. This was the 40 et 8's parade as it passed Cathedral Square. (Library)

LEGIONNAIRES TOOK OVER Wisconsin Avenue during one of the wildest few days in the city's history. There were 57,000 delegates in town, along with their families, and they were joined downtown by Milwaukeeans who wanted to be where the action was. The hotel room shortage, chronic in Milwaukee since the first Yankees showed up and moved in with Solomon Juneau, forced many visitors to room in private homes. That didn't matter much. They seldom went to bed anyway. (Journal)

MAYOR CARL ZEIDLER, a Republican who ended the twenty-six-year regime of Socialist Dan Hoan in 1940, returned to his city hall office for a visit in 1942 after getting a Navy commission. A few months later, his ship was torpedoed by a German submarine off South Africa. All hands were lost. (Journal)

JOHN L. BOHN (right) succeeded Carl Zeidler as mayor. In 1948, when Bohn retired, Frank Zeidler, brother of Carl, won the office, serving for twelve years. One of Bohn's duties was to serve a piece of birthday cake to John G. Gregory, author of a four-volume history of Milwaukee. (Library)

AFTER PEARL HARBOR, civilians were urged to aid the war effort by investing in Victory Bonds. Victory stamps, which could be traded for bonds when enough were accumulated, were sold at playgrounds by a "Victory truck." (Muni. Rec.)

THE MILWAUKEE YACHT CLUB'S headquarters on the lake front burned on November 23, 1943. (Library)

WITH GASOLINE and tires rationed, the electric interurban lines handled increased numbers of Milwaukee commuters and shoppers. This was the Waukesha Local. (Library)

FOUR-FOOTED HORSEPOWER also made a modest comeback during the war. Oscar Solochek, a junk dealer, made his rounds on a rainy afternoon without having to worry about fuel rationing for his vehicle. (Journal)

AFTER AMERICAN VICTORIES in Africa and Europe, German prisoners began arriving in Milwaukee and several other Wisconsin cities. These men are among the one thousand who were housed in a prison compound at General Mitchell Field, where they assembled batteries used in training U.S. troops. Germans found prison life relatively pleasant in a region where so many residents could speak their language. Some returned to Milwaukee after the war. (Journal)

MOST YOUNGER MEN were gone, so it was up to those left behind to keep up the traditions at such affairs as the South Division Civic Association picnic, held in the summer of 1945. In the front row are William George Bruce, a newspaperman and author turned book publisher, Mayor Bohn, and industrialist Charles I. Wesley, who was host to the gathering at his Lake Pewaukee home. (Library)

GERTIE THE DUCK gained a place in Milwaukee's heart by hatching her family on a piling in the river just south of the Wisconsin Avenue Bridge. Nearly everyone in town came to see this mallard celebrity at least once, and some came every day. The river was flushed out with lake water to make it clean enough for Gertie. Trolley cars stopped on the bridge to give passengers a glimpse. Milwaukeeans sent her Mother's Day cards. A children's book was written about her. Gertie's adventures, which ended happily when she and her family got a police escort to Juneau Park lagoon, were exhaustively chronicled in the newspapers, a welcome relief from the war news in April of 1945. (Journal)

THE OLD THIRD WARD, once Irish, had become predominately Italian by the 1940s. Social life was centered around the Madonna Di Pompeii Catholic Church, where festivals like this began. (Library)

JOSEPH R. McCARTHY (right), who had worked his way through Marquette University in Milwaukee, upset Bob La Follette, Jr., in the 1946 Republican primary and went on to become one of the most controversial senators in American history. He is shown with Sen. Everett Dirksen of Illinois shortly after arriving in Washington. (Library)

THE GREEN BAY PACKERS, seeking to stay solvent during the Depression, began playing some of their home games in Milwaukee. The custom continued after the hard times ended. In this 1949 photo, Elroy "Crazy Legs" Hirsch is being tackled by Packer center Jay Rhodemyre. A former star halfback at Wisconsin, Hirsch was playing for the Rams. He later became UW's athletic director. (Journal)

THAT CUTE LITTLE FELlow being held by Walter J. Kessler (right) is Samson, who grew into the largest gorilla in captivity and the best known resident of the Milwaukee zoo. Rudolph C. Zimmerman, another Pabst Brewery official, is holding Sambo, also acquired in 1950. (Journal)

THE WORST TRAFFIC TIE-UP in local history resulted from an eighteen-inch snow accompanied by sixty-mile-per-hour winds on January 29 and 30, 1947. This stranded trolley on South Second was one of thousands of abandoned vehicles after the storm. (Library)

[137]

BEVERLY GEIGER got out her skis when she looked out after the storm of '47 to find drifts were nearly as high as the house. It took a week to dig out Milwaukee so traffic could move normally again. (Journal)

WORLD WAR II delayed the start of television broadcasting. Milwaukee's first station, WTMJ-TV, went on the air December 3, 1947. Most sets were in taverns at first, but one was installed at Seifert Social Center for lads too young to belly up to a bar. (Muni. Rec.)

THE COLD WAR with Russia began almost as soon as the hot war with Germany and Japan ended. There were urgent official suggestions to build bomb shelters or find secure hiding places in case Moscow chose to bomb Milwaukee. Zoo director George Speidel decided the safest place in town was this shelter under a rocky hill built for African wild sheep called aoudads. (Zoo)

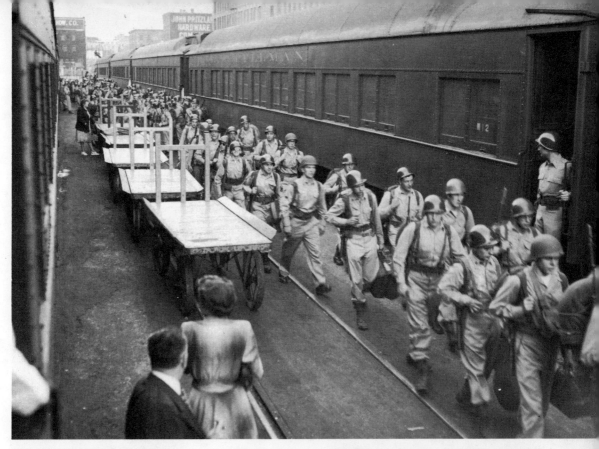

THE UNITED NATIONS' "police action" in Korea, with Americans doing most of the fighting, brought a revival of scenes like this at the Milwaukee Road Station. (Library)

GEN. DOUGLAS MacARTHUR hadn't been back for half a century when he arrived in Milwaukee for a triumphant homecoming after being relieved of command in Korea by President Truman. As the most famous ex-Milwaukeean of his day, he drew one of the biggest turnouts in local history. (Library)

THIS IS A SMALL PORTION of the crowd that turned out to see MacArthur. One of his appearances was here in Marquette Stadium, once the scene of college football games. County Stadium had not yet been built. (Pabst)

MacARTHUR'S MOTORCADE left some hard feelings behind, speeding past spectators so fast it was hard to get a good look at the general. In his speech to Congress, he had said that old soldiers never die, they only fade away. MacArthur was the symbol of a period in history and an attitude of mind that were already fading. His departure from the scene marked the end of an era. (Pabst)

Index